Guided by Grace

SETTING AND ACHIEVING GOALS WITH GOD

TAMARA K. ANDERSON

Daily Hope Publishing

Guided by Grace: Setting and Achieving Goals with God
Copyright © Tamara K. Anderson 2024

All rights reserved. No part of this publication may be reproduced or transmitted in any form or by any means electronic or mechanical, including photocopy, recording, or any information storage and retrieval system now known or to be invented, without permission in writing from the publisher, except by a reviewer who wishes to quote brief passages in connection with a review written for inclusion in a magazine, newspaper, website, or broadcast.

If you want to use any of this material, please contact the publisher for permission through the website **tamarakanderson.com**.

Published by Day Hope Publishing

All the scriptural verses shared in this book are from the King James Version of the Bible.

Book cover and interior design by Francine Eden Platt
Eden Graphics, Inc. • www.edengraphics.net

Image sources: Pricilla du Preez, Neom, Nic-Chi, and Robin Schreiner at Unsplash.com; and Cobalt88 at istockphoto.com

ISBN 978-1-7321469-5-2

Published in the United States by Daily Hope Publishing

Manufactured in the United States of America
10 9 8 7 6 5 4 3 2 1

TABLE OF CONTENTS

Introduction 1
Build the List 2
Prayers, Answers, and Decisions 3
    Prayers 3
    Answers 4
    Decisions 5
Commitment and Action 6
Investing in Myself and My Goal 7
Build Trust with God 8

Goal Setting Tips & Hacks 11
    Brainstorming & Understanding 12
    Understand Your WHY 13
    Considering the Details 14
    Goal Setting Specifics 15
    The Power of Rewarding Yourself 16
    Reward Ideas 17
    NOT-To-Do List – Example 20
    NOT-To-Do List Exercise 21
    7 Levels Deep WHY Exercise – Example 28
    7 Levels Deep WHY Exercise 29
    7 Levels Deep Overcoming Fear – Example 36
    7 Levels Deep Overcoming Fear Exercise 37

Goal Setting Worksheets 51
    Worksheet Instructions 52
    First Quarter Weekly Goals / Obstacles / Summaries / Notes 53
    Second Quarter Weekly Goals / Obstacles / Summaries / Notes 133
    Third Quarter Weekly Goals / Obstacles / Summaries / Notes 213
    Fourth Quarter Weekly Goals / Obstacles / Summaries / Notes 293
    End of Year Summary 372

About the Author 394

DEDICATION

To God, for giving me the wisdom, strength, and courage to accomplish the impossible.

And to you, my faithful friend, for trusting God to guide you on your journey to soar to greater heights.

INTRODUCTION

Is anything too hard for the Lord?
GENESIS 18:14

I love this verse! It is even better when you remember its context—this is what was said to Sarah (of Abraham and Sarah) when they were told she would have a son, long after her child-bearing years were over. And guess what? She did. She had Isaac when she was in her nineties.

The reason I love this verse is because it reminds me **nothing is impossible with God's help**, if it is according to His will.

When you commit to setting goals with God, you open the door to miracles in your life—because nothing is **"too hard for the Lord."**

So, let's take a journey together and watch miracles unfold!

BUILD THE LIST

*I will instruct thee and teach thee in the way
which thou shalt go: I will guide thee with mine eye.*

PSALM 32:8

FIRST THINGS FIRST: Make a list of everything you can imagine or dream of doing this year. This may take more than one day. That is okay. You aren't in a rush. Keep thinking and jotting down ideas as they come to you. You can even have a chat with God about helping you make a good list. Begin your list TODAY!!!

Questions to help you think:
- What have I talked about doing for years?
- What is meaningful to me, or what am I passionate about?
- What goal would give me purpose?
- What would make me feel a sense of accomplishment this year?
- What talent would I like to develop?
- What would I like to become, and what skills would take me there?
- What do I need to carry out Spiritually? Physically? Emotionally? Socially? Family? At work?

PRAYERS, ANSWERS, AND DECISIONS

PRAYER

If any of you lack wisdom, let him ask of God.

JAMES 1:5

Now comes the part where you talk to God about your choices. He is your Father, and like any good father, He cares about you and wants to see you reach your full potential. *"The Spirit itself beareth witness with our spirit, that **we are the children of God**."* – Romans 8:16

1. **Find a quiet place you can meditate (deeply reflect) and pray.**

    "When thou prayest, enter into thy closet, and when thou has shut the door, pray to thy Father which is in secret; and thy Father which seeth in secret shall reward thee openly." – Matthew 6:6

2. **Begin by addressing God as your Father.**

    "After this manner therefore pray ye: Our Father which art in heaven, Hallowed be thy name." – Matthew 6:9

3. **Thank God for your blessings.**

    "It is a good thing to give thanks unto the Lord." – Psalm 92:1

4. **Talk to Him about your list,** how you desire to commit to one thing, ask Him for guidance and to recognize when He answers you.

    "Ask and ye shall receive." – John 16:24

5. **Close in the name of Jesus Christ.**

    *"Whatsoever ye shall ask the Father **in my name**, he will give it you."* – John 16:23

You may or may not get immediate ideas, impressions, and answers. Read on to determine your next step in receiving answers.

ANSWERS

The Spirit of truth will guide you into all truth.

JOHN 16:13

God speaks to each of us, and we need to learn to hear and recognize His voice. Ask Him to help you realize when He is speaking to you. Here are some things to remember during this process:

- **God's Own Timing:** Remember God will give you answers in His own time and in His own way, and only according to His will. *"Thy will be done in earth, as it is in heaven"* (Matthew 6:10). Don't get discouraged if you don't receive an immediate answer. Keep trying.

- **A Quiet Answer:** Sometimes God answers with thoughts and impressions in the mind—kind of like a *light-bulb moment*. Elijah described this as a *"still small voice… and, behold, there came a voice unto him and said, What doest thou here, Elijah?"* (1 Kings 19:12, 13). Pay attention to your *light bulb moments* or thoughts and write them down. God just might be speaking to you.

- **Distractions & Solutions:** Often, we must wade through distractions before we finally hear or feel a quiet voice in our heart and mind, teaching or prompting us one way or another. If you are feeling distracted try these things:
    - Turn off your cell phone/TV or other digital devices.
    - Create quiet times in your life (this is particularly effective in early morning).
    - Resolve issues that may hinder your answer (forgive yourself and others, let go of hurt feelings, apologize for your own offenses, cast out negative emotions in the name of Jesus and invite in positivity and peace).
    - Take a quiet walk in nature (no phone or other distractions).
    - Visit a holy or quiet place where you can think (church, in nature).
    - Make a quiet place/time to ponder without interruptions in your home.

- **Ponder, Decide, then Ask:** Sometimes God wants us to think about our options, maybe even make a pro/con list, decide, and then ask Him if our decision is correct. As we go through this process we become more invested, and we learn and grow.
    - **Feeling Peace:** If it is right, you will feel peace or assurance. Peace is one of the *"fruits of the spirit"* as described by the apostle Paul. *"The fruit of the Spirit is love, joy, peace, longsuffering, gentleness, goodness, faith, meekness, temperance"* (Galatians 5:22–23). These are feelings that mean, *Yes. I love you. Keep going. Proceed.*
    - **Feeling Uncertain:** If the decision or answer is wrong, you will feel confused or uncertain. This is the opposite of peace. Sometimes I feel like I have a big knot in my stomach. I will often verify I am understanding God correctly and ask the question a different way. For example, "I feel like this is not the right choice, is that correct?" Then if I then feel peace I know I as getting the right answer.
    - **Ask for Help:** Sometimes I ask a family member or trusted spiritual friend to pray for me to receive guidance, or to pray with me to see if they can help me make sense of my answer.

- **No Clear Answer?** There are also times when God trusts you to decide, so move forward knowing He will tell you to stop or change something as you proceed forward with faith.

DECISION

By prayer and supplication with THANKSGIVING *let your requests be made known unto God. And the* PEACE OF GOD, *which passeth all understanding, shall keep your hearts and minds* THROUGH CHRIST JESUS.

PHILIPPIANS 4:6-7

What answer did I receive? What goal will I be setting?

___

How do I feel about this answer?

___

If I feel fear, how do I believe God will strengthen me and mercifully help me to accomplish this goal?

___

COMMITMENT AND ACTION

Once you make a decision, the universe conspires to make it happen.
RALPH WALDO EMERSON

My Inspired Resolution — At the end of your commitment sentence below write, 'with God's help.' For example, "I commit to write my personal history this year *with God's help*."

I commit to: _____

_____

What makes me excited about this goal? _____

_____

How will this goal improve me as a person? _____

_____

How will I feel when I accomplish this goal? _____

_____

What scares me about this goal? _____

_____

What obstacles do I foresee? _____

_____

_____

Brainstorm how to overcome those obstacles. _____

_____

_____

INVESTING IN MYSELF AND MY GOAL

All that the Lord hath said will He do.

EXODUS 24:7

What resources (time, money, skills, education) do I need to accomplish this goal? _____

_____
_____
_____
_____
_____

Would my goal be easier with a mentor or an accountability group? If so, who can help and support/mentor me in this goal? If you don't know, ask God to help you figure this out or ask friends or others on social media if they can recommend a good mentor.

_____
_____
_____
_____
_____
_____

When will I commit to work on this goal? Write days of the week and brainstorm times. _____

_____
_____

Don't worry if you aren't completely sure how to fit working on your goal in yet. Begin thinking about it. There is a 'Not-To-Do List' hack we will work on later, to help you make more time for what is most important.

If God be for us, who can be against us?

ROMANS 8:31

BUILD TRUST WITH GOD

After ye were illuminated, ye endured a great fight of afflictions; . . . Cast not away therefore your confidence, which hath a great recompense of reward.

HEBREWS 10:32,35

Through any journey with God, we each learn the principle of trusting Him completely. This is so much easier said than done, especially when doubts creep in. I love the Bible verse above; to not cast away our initial confidence when the adversary tries to get us to give up on our goal. It is a mental battle.

- **Closed Doors:** When the Children of Israel left Egypt and came to the Red Sea, they suddenly felt panic and fear. That can happen to us as well—following God's path, only to find a closed door. We may feel trapped and unsure of what to do next.
    - **Personal Example:** I submitted my book manuscript to two different publishing companies. Both replied with rejection letters. I felt discouraged and stuck because I knew I'd been guided by God to publish my story. I put my book on the backburner, while I figured out what God wanted me to do next.
    - **Briefly share a story** of a time when God closed a door you were going to go through.

_____
_____
_____
_____

- **Opening New Door:** The Children of Israel were amazed when God parted the Red Sea, and they knew only the power of God could do such a thing. It was another miracle on their journey, but one they never could have imagined. God can miraculously open unseen doors for you, too.
    - **Personal Example:** My closed doors eventually led me to the right door I needed to go through. I met Richard Paul Evans and began a training and mentoring program with him and his staff. The result? I published my book!
    - **Share a story** of when a different door or opportunity opened to you in your life.

_____
_____
_____
_____

- **Submitting & Doing Hard Things:** Jesus Christ is our ultimate example of submitting our will to His and trusting the path laid before us. While suffering in Gethsemane He said, "O my Father, if it be possible, let this cup pass from me: nevertheless not as I will, but as thou wilt" (Matthew 26:39).

  - **Personal Example:** When my son Nathan was diagnosed with autism, an incurable and lifelong disease, I was sure God could heal him if I had enough faith. But after many months of prayer, I had to learn to change my prayer and submit to God's will—even though I knew raising a child with a disability would be so very hard. I had to walk with God through something that was too hard for me to do on my own, and He opened the way by helping me solve challenges—one at a time.

  - **Share about a time when** you or someone you love had to submit to God's will, walk through hard times, and what was learned through the process.

Continue walking with God through each obstacle. As you navigate each challenge, you will build increasing trust, and come to know that when you are yoked to Him, you can accomplish anything.

TRUST IN THE LORD *with all thine heart; and lean not unto thine own understanding. In all thy ways acknowledge Him, and* HE SHALL DIRECT THY PATHS.

PROVERBS 3:5-6

GOAL SETTING
Tips & Hacks

GOAL SETTING TIPS & HACKS

Do you want to increase your chances of accomplishing your goal? If so, here are a few hacks which will help you write goals that you can both measure and achieve.

I received my Bachelor of Science degree in Therapeutic Recreation. We had an entire course on how to write measurable goals for the clients we would work with. I am going to share with you a few of the key tips I learned decades ago which are still applicable when setting and reaching goals today.

BRAINSTORMING & UNDERSTANDING

Take a moment to consider some of these questions and write your thoughts in the space below.

- Which goal do I aim to accomplish?
- Do I have the control and capacity to do it? Make sure your personal goals are something you can achieve, and not wholly dependent on someone else. You only have control over yourself.
- Who do I need to become to achieve this goal?
- Which changes will I need to make?
- Which things might I need to give up?

HACK: Use **Not-To-Do List** as needed, which will be explained later in this section.

UNDERSTANDING YOUR 'WHY'

Why is it important to me that I accomplish this goal?

_____

_____

_____

_____

_____

It is necessary to have your sights set on your why to help pull you through the fear and obstacles you will likely face through the process.

For example, when I was facing the fear of starting a podcast, God taught me that I needed to keep my eye on Him and allow faith to overcome fear. When I was in the sixth grade I was often bullied, and that pain stayed with me for years, resurfacing when I wanted to start podcasting. If I had fallen back on those experiences, I would have stayed stuck in past fears and never had the courage to move forward. But with God's help, I found the resources I needed to not only figure out what was holding me back, but to face it and move forward in faith.

HACK: 7 Levels Deep WHY Exercise, which will be in the next few pages.

HACK: 7 Levels Deep Overcoming Fear, which will be explained in the coming pages.

How will I feel when I accomplish my goal?

_____

_____

_____

_____

_____

The Lord will perfect that which concerneth me: THY MERCY,
O Lord, ENDURETH FOR EVER: *forsake not the works of thine own hands.*

PSALM 138:8

CONSIDERING THE DETAILS

What are the necessary steps I can see for this goal?

What is the first step?

What resources do I already have to help me move forward? (people, skills, personal attributes, books, courses, information, financial backing, etc.)

What resources do I need to accomplish this goal?

Do I need a mentor? An online course? An accountability group? More schooling?

Who can help me?

GOAL SETTING SPECIFICS

One key to setting measurable, reachable goals, is the ability to track your progress so specifically, there is no doubt when you have accomplished that goal.

Questions to Ask:
- What exactly do I want to achieve?
- What will I do?
- When will I work on my goal?

Add Measurable Parameters:
- Add 'by a certain time' deadlines or target finish dates.
- Add a minimum/maximum amount of time you will work on the goal daily, weekly, etc.
- Add a measurable number of times, days, hours, emails, calls, percentages, or checkpoints to each mini goal.

For example, if I simply say, "I will write and publish a book," I might imagine that I will finish the book, but there are no specifics, and no deadlines. I need to add numbers and break it down to a weekly goal.

A more specific and measurable goal would be, "I will write thirty minutes to an hour each day, four days this week, right after my kids leave for school."

Ultimate big goal deadline: "I will publish my book on April 2, 2025 on World Autism Awareness Day."

Now it is your turn to practice writing your big goal and some mini-goals with measurable parameters.

_____

_____

_____

_____

_____

_____

_____

_____

THE POWER OF REWARDING YOURSELF

And whatsoever ye do, do it heartily...
Knowing that of the Lord ye shall receive the reward.

COLOSSIANS 3:23-24

It is important to reward yourself when you achieve small milestones on your journey. Because working on goals can be hard, small wins can boost motivation, enhance self-confidence, focus, and ultimately propel you towards greater success.

Recently, I had a list of five things I had to get done by lunchtime. Some of these items were not very fun to do, so I decided to reward myself. Reading has always been my escape so I said, *"I will read one-hour guilt-free when I am finished."* This was the perfect motivation for me. I accomplished my goal and got to read for an hour!

It was a win-win situation. I moved forward with my daily goals, built momentum, plus I gave myself a reward. It was a happy day!

What is your preferred way to reward yourself? I have one child who loves rewards that involve food, another who loves physical contact like hugs and social interactions, and one who lives for video game time. My husband likes going on adventures and revels in praise when he has completed a task. I prefer playing board games, hanging with friends, or reading. Each of will choose different ways of rewarding ourselves.

Some goals will be small, and some larger. You will need to choose varying degrees of rewards that correspond to the particular goal.

My specific goal might look like this, with a reward at the end: "I will write thirty minutes to an hour each day, four days this week, right after my kids leave for school. My daily reward will be *'listen to my audiobook for thirty minutes'*. My weekly reward will be *'go to lunch with a friend.'*

Rewards I enjoy or would like to try:

_____
_____
_____
_____

Practice writing your goals and add rewards:

_____
_____
_____
_____

REWARD IDEAS

Here are some reward ideas. Circle the rewards you like and brainstorm more.

- Take a warm bath
- Have breakfast in bed
- Get a massage
- Sit in a sauna
- Buy yourself a flower
- Go to a pet store and play with animals
- Walk a scenic path
- Visit a zoo
- Have a manicure or a pedicure
- Smell some flowers
- Watch the sunrise or sunset
- Relax with a good book
- Listen to soothing music
- Watch a funny movie
- Dance to your favorite music
- Go to bed early
- Sleep outside under the stars
- Take a 'mental health day' off
- Eat by candlelight
- Go for a walk
- Call a good friend
- Eat out at a fine restaurant
- Go to the beach
- Take a scenic drive
- Meditate
- Do Yoga or other favorite exercise
- Sit on the porch
- Browse in a book or music store
- Buy yourself a stuffed animal
- Write yourself a love letter and mail it
- Write in your journal
- Buy yourself something special (and affordable)
- Watch a good movie or show
- Swing on a swing
- Visit a museum
- Let yourself window shop
- Work on a favorite puzzle
- Sit in a hot tub
- Read ___ pages in an inspirational book
- Write a letter to an old friend
- Spend time near a river, stream or creek
- Hold a baby
- Dry your hair in the sunshine

- Pot some plants and get muddy
- Sit in a circle of trees
- Dress up nicely
- Play a game
- Do hand work (knit, crochet, etc.)
- Play a musical instrument
- Look at old photos
- Play a favorite sport
- Solve a riddle
- Think about a happy time in your life and write about it
- Go to the mountains
- Do something new
- Find a service opportunity and do it
- Go for a horseback ride
- Go to an aquarium
- Take a dance class
- Go to lunch with a friend
- Tell yourself "good job" for something you've done
- Picnic by yourself or with a friend
- Look in the mirror and say, "I love you!"
- Write 10+ good qualities you have
- Buy a new book (or check one out at the library)
- Go water or snow skiing
- Go bowling
- Do woodwork
- Go sailing
- Plan a trip
- Paint
- Do something spontaneous
- Take a nap
- Go hammocking
- Join a club
- Take a child somewhere
- Clean or organize something for enjoyment
- Go on an airplane ride
- Spend time alone
- Do some acting
- Do something fun with a child
- Invite a friend to walk with you
- Take some photos
- Watch a sports game in person
- Sing by yourself or in a group
- Laugh and have fun
- Do arts or crafts
- Cook something delicious
- Start a collection (shells, coins, leaves…)
- Buy a gift
- Go for a bike ride

- Daydream
- Write 10+ things you are grateful for
- Write a poem, article, book....
- Sew
- Go to dinner with friends
- Sightsee
- Garden
- Read a newspaper or magazine article
- Kiss
- Go on a date
- Relax--do nothing
- Go to a movie
- Buy a gadget
- Spend time in the sun
- Plan a reunion or party
- Write 5 positive affirmations
- Pray
- Arrange flowers
- Sing like you are on stage
- Go camping
- Run or jog
- Ride a motorbike
- Fly a kite
- Do a hobby
- Learn to fly a drone
- Put money aside for a future dream
- Plan a day of activities
- Meet someone new
- Eat something yummy
- Learn some karate moves
- Repair something around your home
- Take care of plants or visit a greenhouse
- Go swimming
- Doodle
- Listen to an audiobook
- Collect memorial things from your past
- Attend a party or get-together
- Plan your next big purchase
- Play golf or putt-putt
- Watch children play
- Go on a hike
- Go to a play or concert
- Refinish or reupholster some furniture
- Redecorate a room
- Visit a second hand store
- Donate something
- Travel to a state or national park
- Hang a bird feeder or go bird watching
- Go to a lake
- Invite a new friend to lunch

NOT-TO-DO LIST — EXAMPLE

DATE: _3/5/21_

Do you need more time to accomplish what is most important? This 'not-to-do list' is more important than a 'to-do' list as it will help you figure out what you should NOT be spending your time on. Pray and ask God to help you with this process. You can also brainstorm with a trusted friend to help you find ways to free up time to work on your goals.

List the actions you spend time on:

1. Record Podcasts
2. Edit Podcasts
3. Record w/ Brad & Joy
4. Accountability Calls
5. Social Media
6. Music & Voice
7. Self-Reliance Class
8. Cooking — Kids 1 day wk / Buy 1 day wk / ex: Pot. Soup
9.
10.

Circle one of the following for each:

1. Automate   Delegate   Eliminate   Change   **(Keep)**
2. Automate   Delegate ? Eliminate   Change   **(Keep)**
3. Automate   Delegate   **(Eliminate)**   Change   Keep
4. Automate   Delegate   Eliminate   Change   **(Keep)**
5. **(Automate)**   Delegate   Eliminate   **(Change)**   Keep
6. Automate   Delegate   Eliminate   Change   **(Keep)**
7. Automate   Delegate   Eliminate   Change   **(Keep)**
8. Automate   Delegate   Eliminate   **(Change)**   Keep
9. Automate   Delegate   Eliminate   Change   Keep
10. Automate   Delegate   Eliminate   Change   Keep

What are the top 3 actions that move the needle the most in my life?

✳ Women Warriors of Light

Book Donations

Podcasts

What are the top 3 things I must eliminate or change first in my life?

Record w/ Brad & Joy

Social Media

Cooking - simplify

NOT-TO-DO LIST — EXERCISE

DATE: _____

Do you need more time to accomplish what is most important? This 'not-to-do list' is more important than a 'to-do' list as it will help you figure out what you should NOT be spending your time on. Pray and ask God to help you with this process. You can also brainstorm with a trusted friend to help you find ways to free up time to work on your goals.

List the actions you spend time on:

1. _____
2. _____
3. _____
4. _____
5. _____
6. _____
7. _____
8. _____
9. _____
10. _____

Circle one of the following for each:

1. Automate   Delegate   Eliminate   Change   Keep
2. Automate   Delegate   Eliminate   Change   Keep
3. Automate   Delegate   Eliminate   Change   Keep
4. Automate   Delegate   Eliminate   Change   Keep
5. Automate   Delegate   Eliminate   Change   Keep
6. Automate   Delegate   Eliminate   Change   Keep
7. Automate   Delegate   Eliminate   Change   Keep
8. Automate   Delegate   Eliminate   Change   Keep
9. Automate   Delegate   Eliminate   Change   Keep
10. Automate   Delegate   Eliminate   Change   Keep

What are the top 3 actions that move the needle the most in my life?

_____
_____
_____

What are the top 3 things I must eliminate or change first in my life?

_____
_____
_____

NOT-TO-DO LIST — EXERCISE

DATE: _____

Do you need more time to accomplish what is most important? This 'not-to-do list' is more important than a 'to-do' list as it will help you figure out what you should NOT be spending your time on. Pray and ask God to help you with this process. You can also brainstorm with a trusted friend to help you find ways to free up time to work on your goals.

List the actions you spend time on:

1. _____
2. _____
3. _____
4. _____
5. _____
6. _____
7. _____
8. _____
9. _____
10. _____

Circle one of the following for each:

1. Automate   Delegate   Eliminate   Change   Keep
2. Automate   Delegate   Eliminate   Change   Keep
3. Automate   Delegate   Eliminate   Change   Keep
4. Automate   Delegate   Eliminate   Change   Keep
5. Automate   Delegate   Eliminate   Change   Keep
6. Automate   Delegate   Eliminate   Change   Keep
7. Automate   Delegate   Eliminate   Change   Keep
8. Automate   Delegate   Eliminate   Change   Keep
9. Automate   Delegate   Eliminate   Change   Keep
10. Automate   Delegate   Eliminate   Change   Keep

What are the top 3 actions that move the needle the most in my life?

_____
_____
_____

What are the top 3 things I must eliminate or change first in my life?

_____
_____
_____

NOT-TO-DO LIST — EXERCISE

DATE: _____

Do you need more time to accomplish what is most important? This 'not-to-do list' is more important than a 'to-do' list as it will help you figure out what you should NOT be spending your time on. Pray and ask God to help you with this process. You can also brainstorm with a trusted friend to help you find ways to free up time to work on your goals.

List the actions you spend time on:

1. _____
2. _____
3. _____
4. _____
5. _____
6. _____
7. _____
8. _____
9. _____
10. _____

Circle one of the following for each:

1. Automate   Delegate   Eliminate   Change   Keep
2. Automate   Delegate   Eliminate   Change   Keep
3. Automate   Delegate   Eliminate   Change   Keep
4. Automate   Delegate   Eliminate   Change   Keep
5. Automate   Delegate   Eliminate   Change   Keep
6. Automate   Delegate   Eliminate   Change   Keep
7. Automate   Delegate   Eliminate   Change   Keep
8. Automate   Delegate   Eliminate   Change   Keep
9. Automate   Delegate   Eliminate   Change   Keep
10. Automate   Delegate   Eliminate   Change   Keep

What are the top 3 actions that move the needle the most in my life?

_____
_____
_____

What are the top 3 things I must eliminate or change first in my life?

_____
_____
_____

NOT-TO-DO LIST — EXERCISE

DATE: _____

Do you need more time to accomplish what is most important? This 'not-to-do list' is more important than a 'to-do' list as it will help you figure out what you should NOT be spending your time on. Pray and ask God to help you with this process. You can also brainstorm with a trusted friend to help you find ways to free up time to work on your goals.

List the actions you spend time on:

1. _____
2. _____
3. _____
4. _____
5. _____
6. _____
7. _____
8. _____
9. _____
10. _____

Circle one of the following for each:

1. Automate   Delegate   Eliminate   Change   Keep
2. Automate   Delegate   Eliminate   Change   Keep
3. Automate   Delegate   Eliminate   Change   Keep
4. Automate   Delegate   Eliminate   Change   Keep
5. Automate   Delegate   Eliminate   Change   Keep
6. Automate   Delegate   Eliminate   Change   Keep
7. Automate   Delegate   Eliminate   Change   Keep
8. Automate   Delegate   Eliminate   Change   Keep
9. Automate   Delegate   Eliminate   Change   Keep
10. Automate   Delegate   Eliminate   Change   Keep

What are the top 3 actions that move the needle the most in my life?

_____

_____

_____

What are the top 3 things I must eliminate or change first in my life?

_____

_____

_____

NOT-TO-DO LIST — EXERCISE

DATE: _____

Do you need more time to accomplish what is most important? This 'not-to-do list' is more important than a 'to-do' list as it will help you figure out what you should NOT be spending your time on. Pray and ask God to help you with this process. You can also brainstorm with a trusted friend to help you find ways to free up time to work on your goals.

List the actions you spend time on:

1. _____
2. _____
3. _____
4. _____
5. _____
6. _____
7. _____
8. _____
9. _____
10. _____

Circle one of the following for each:

1. Automate   Delegate   Eliminate   Change   Keep
2. Automate   Delegate   Eliminate   Change   Keep
3. Automate   Delegate   Eliminate   Change   Keep
4. Automate   Delegate   Eliminate   Change   Keep
5. Automate   Delegate   Eliminate   Change   Keep
6. Automate   Delegate   Eliminate   Change   Keep
7. Automate   Delegate   Eliminate   Change   Keep
8. Automate   Delegate   Eliminate   Change   Keep
9. Automate   Delegate   Eliminate   Change   Keep
10. Automate   Delegate   Eliminate   Change   Keep

What are the top 3 actions that move the needle the most in my life?

_____

_____

_____

What are the top 3 things I must eliminate or change first in my life?

_____

_____

_____

NOT-TO-DO LIST — EXERCISE

DATE: _____

Do you need more time to accomplish what is most important? This 'not-to-do list' is more important than a 'to-do' list as it will help you figure out what you should NOT be spending your time on. Pray and ask God to help you with this process. You can also brainstorm with a trusted friend to help you find ways to free up time to work on your goals.

List the actions you spend time on:

1. _____
2. _____
3. _____
4. _____
5. _____
6. _____
7. _____
8. _____
9. _____
10. _____

Circle one of the following for each:

1. Automate   Delegate   Eliminate   Change   Keep
2. Automate   Delegate   Eliminate   Change   Keep
3. Automate   Delegate   Eliminate   Change   Keep
4. Automate   Delegate   Eliminate   Change   Keep
5. Automate   Delegate   Eliminate   Change   Keep
6. Automate   Delegate   Eliminate   Change   Keep
7. Automate   Delegate   Eliminate   Change   Keep
8. Automate   Delegate   Eliminate   Change   Keep
9. Automate   Delegate   Eliminate   Change   Keep
10. Automate   Delegate   Eliminate   Change   Keep

What are the top 3 actions that move the needle the most in my life?

_____
_____
_____

What are the top 3 things I must eliminate or change first in my life?

_____
_____
_____

NOT-TO-DO LIST — EXERCISE

DATE: _____

Do you need more time to accomplish what is most important? This 'not-to-do list' is more important than a 'to-do' list as it will help you figure out what you should NOT be spending your time on. Pray and ask God to help you with this process. You can also brainstorm with a trusted friend to help you find ways to free up time to work on your goals.

List the actions you spend time on:

1. _____
2. _____
3. _____
4. _____
5. _____
6. _____
7. _____
8. _____
9. _____
10. _____

Circle one of the following for each:

1. Automate   Delegate   Eliminate   Change   Keep
2. Automate   Delegate   Eliminate   Change   Keep
3. Automate   Delegate   Eliminate   Change   Keep
4. Automate   Delegate   Eliminate   Change   Keep
5. Automate   Delegate   Eliminate   Change   Keep
6. Automate   Delegate   Eliminate   Change   Keep
7. Automate   Delegate   Eliminate   Change   Keep
8. Automate   Delegate   Eliminate   Change   Keep
9. Automate   Delegate   Eliminate   Change   Keep
10. Automate   Delegate   Eliminate   Change   Keep

What are the top 3 actions that move the needle the most in my life?

_____
_____
_____

What are the top 3 things I must eliminate or change first in my life?

_____
_____
_____

7 Levels Deep WHY – EXAMPLE

The 7 Levels Deep Exercise can be used to help determine what really drives you to accomplish anything in life and find your deepest level why.

INSTRUCTIONS: Be completely open and honest with yourself in this exercise. Turn the answer from the previous level into the next question.

DATE: 3/5/21

LEVEL 1: Why is it important for me to set this new goal?

I want to share my message with people so they know they're not alone.

LEVEL 2: Why is it important for me to help others know they're not alone?

Because it is so awful and isolating to feel like no one understands.

LEVEL 3: Why is it important for me to help people feel understood?

Because then they will feel hope and validation.

LEVEL 4: Why is it important for me to help people feel hope?

Because then they won't give up and keep going during hard times.

LEVEL 5: Why is it important for me to help people keep going?

Because life's burdens seem easier when they are shared.

LEVEL 6: Why is it important for me to share burdens?

Because sharing my burden with God saved me in my darkest moment.

LEVEL 7: Why is it important for me to share burdens with God?

Because I am not strong enough to carry my burdens on my own.

My WHY: *I want to point people to God to help carry their burdens because it is too hard on their own, and I want them to feel hope and keep going.*

7 Levels Deep WHY — EXERCISE

The 7 Levels Deep Exercise can be used to help determine what really drives you to accomplish anything in life and find your deepest level why.

INSTRUCTIONS: Be completely open and honest with yourself in this exercise. Turn the answer from the previous level into the next question.

DATE: _____

LEVEL 1: Why is it important for me to set this new goal?

_____

LEVEL 2: Why is it important for me to _____

_____

LEVEL 3: Why is it important for me to _____

_____

LEVEL 4: Why is it important for me to _____

_____

LEVEL 5: Why is it important for me to _____

_____

LEVEL 6: Why is it important for me to _____

_____

LEVEL 7: Why is it important for me to _____

_____

My WHY: _____

_____

7 Levels Deep WHY — EXERCISE

The 7 Levels Deep Exercise can be used to help determine what really drives you to accomplish anything in life and find your deepest level why.

INSTRUCTIONS: Be completely open and honest with yourself in this exercise. Turn the answer from the previous level into the next question.

DATE: _____

LEVEL 1: Why is it important for me to set this new goal?

_____

LEVEL 2: Why is it important for me to _____

_____

LEVEL 3: Why is it important for me to _____

_____

LEVEL 4: Why is it important for me to _____

_____

LEVEL 5: Why is it important for me to _____

_____

LEVEL 6: Why is it important for me to _____

_____

LEVEL 7: Why is it important for me to _____

_____

My WHY: _____

_____

7 Levels Deep WHY — EXERCISE

The 7 Levels Deep Exercise can be used to help determine what really drives you to accomplish anything in life and find your deepest level why.

INSTRUCTIONS: Be completely open and honest with yourself in this exercise. Turn the answer from the previous level into the next question.

DATE: _____

LEVEL 1: Why is it important for me to set this new goal?

_____

LEVEL 2: Why is it important for me to _____

_____

LEVEL 3: Why is it important for me to _____

_____

LEVEL 4: Why is it important for me to _____

_____

LEVEL 5: Why is it important for me to _____

_____

LEVEL 6: Why is it important for me to _____

_____

LEVEL 7: Why is it important for me to _____

_____

My WHY: _____

_____

7 Levels Deep WHY — EXERCISE

The 7 Levels Deep Exercise can be used to help determine what really drives you to accomplish anything in life and find your deepest level why.

INSTRUCTIONS: Be completely open and honest with yourself in this exercise. Turn the answer from the previous level into the next question.

DATE: _____

LEVEL 1: Why is it important for me to set this new goal?

_____

LEVEL 2: Why is it important for me to _____

_____

LEVEL 3: Why is it important for me to _____

_____

LEVEL 4: Why is it important for me to _____

_____

LEVEL 5: Why is it important for me to _____

_____

LEVEL 6: Why is it important for me to _____

_____

LEVEL 7: Why is it important for me to _____

_____

My WHY: _____

_____

7 Levels Deep WHY — EXERCISE

The 7 Levels Deep Exercise can be used to help determine what really drives you to accomplish anything in life and find your deepest level why.

INSTRUCTIONS: Be completely open and honest with yourself in this exercise. Turn the answer from the previous level into the next question.

DATE: _____

LEVEL 1: Why is it important for me to set this new goal?

_____

LEVEL 2: Why is it important for me to _____

_____

LEVEL 3: Why is it important for me to _____

_____

LEVEL 4: Why is it important for me to _____

_____

LEVEL 5: Why is it important for me to _____

_____

LEVEL 6: Why is it important for me to _____

_____

LEVEL 7: Why is it important for me to _____

_____

My WHY: _____

_____

7 Levels Deep WHY — EXERCISE

The 7 Levels Deep Exercise can be used to help determine what really drives you to accomplish anything in life and find your deepest level why.

INSTRUCTIONS: Be completely open and honest with yourself in this exercise. Turn the answer from the previous level into the next question.

DATE: _____

LEVEL 1: Why is it important for me to set this new goal?

_____

LEVEL 2: Why is it important for me to _____

_____

LEVEL 3: Why is it important for me to _____

_____

LEVEL 4: Why is it important for me to _____

_____

LEVEL 5: Why is it important for me to _____

_____

LEVEL 6: Why is it important for me to _____

_____

LEVEL 7: Why is it important for me to _____

_____

My WHY: _____

7 Levels Deep WHY — EXERCISE

The 7 Levels Deep Exercise can be used to help determine what really drives you to accomplish anything in life and find your deepest level why.

INSTRUCTIONS: Be completely open and honest with yourself in this exercise. Turn the answer from the previous level into the next question.

DATE: _____

LEVEL 1: Why is it important for me to set this new goal?

_____

LEVEL 2: Why is it important for me to _____

_____

LEVEL 3: Why is it important for me to _____

_____

LEVEL 4: Why is it important for me to _____

_____

LEVEL 5: Why is it important for me to _____

_____

LEVEL 6: Why is it important for me to _____

_____

LEVEL 7: Why is it important for me to _____

_____

My WHY: _____

_____

7 Levels Deep OVERCOMING FEAR EXAMPLE

The 7 Levels Deep Exercise can be used to help determine what fear is really stopping you and help you weigh the cost and your desires to overcome it.

INSTRUCTIONS: Be completely open and honest with yourself in this exercise. Turn the answer from the previous level into the next question.

MY FEAR   DATE: 10/3/2018

LEVEL 1: What is the fear that is stopping me?
I am scared to launch my podcast.

LEVEL 2: Why *am I scared to launch my podcast?*
I am scared because I have to put myself out there on the World Wide Web.

LEVEL 3: Why *don't I want to be on social media?*
I am scared because I don't enjoy being on social media.

LEVEL 4: Why *don't I enjoy being on social media?*
Because it is a lot of work and if I put myself out there I might be bullied.

LEVEL 5: Why *is the possibility of bullying stopping me?*
Because I was bullied in 6th grade, I was left feeling broken, small, and unimportant.

LEVEL 6: Why *did I feel small and broken when bullied?*
Because I felt like who I was and what I said was unimportant.

LEVEL 7: Why *did I feel my message wasn't important?*
Because I didn't matter.

My Fear: *In 6th grade I decided I didn't matter and my message didn't matter.*
(Side note, I had to journal about this and get it out to help me process it).

Do I want this to stop me? *NO!!! I'm done with this inner belief and ready to let it go!*

My truths: *I matter and my message matters. I have worth. What I say is important and needs to be heard.*

7 Levels Deep OVERCOMING FEAR

The 7 Levels Deep Exercise can be used to help determine what fears are really stopping you, and help weigh the cost and your desire to overcome it.

INSTRUCTIONS: Be completely open and honest with yourself in this exercise. Turn the answer from the previous level into the next question.

MY FEAR   DATE: _____

LEVEL 1: What is the fear that is stopping me?

_____

LEVEL 2: Why _____

_____

LEVEL 3: Why _____

_____

LEVEL 4: Why _____

_____

LEVEL 5: Why _____

_____

LEVEL 6: Why _____

_____

LEVEL 7: Why _____

_____

My Fear: _____

_____

Do I want this to stop me? _____

_____

My truths: _____

_____

7 Levels Deep OVERCOMING FEAR

The 7 Levels Deep Exercise can be used to help determine what fears are really stopping you, and help weigh the cost and your desire to overcome it.

INSTRUCTIONS: Be completely open and honest with yourself in this exercise. Turn the answer from the previous level into the next question.

MY FEAR DATE: _____

LEVEL 1: What is the fear that is stopping me?

_____

LEVEL 2: Why _____

_____

LEVEL 3: Why _____

_____

LEVEL 4: Why _____

_____

LEVEL 5: Why _____

_____

LEVEL 6: Why _____

_____

LEVEL 7: Why _____

_____

My Fear: _____

_____

Do I want this to stop me? _____

_____

My truths: _____

_____

7 Levels Deep OVERCOMING FEAR

The 7 Levels Deep Exercise can be used to help determine what fears are really stopping you, and help weigh the cost and your desire to overcome it.

INSTRUCTIONS: Be completely open and honest with yourself in this exercise. Turn the answer from the previous level into the next question.

MY FEAR   DATE: _____

LEVEL 1: What is the fear that is stopping me?

_____

LEVEL 2: Why _____

_____

LEVEL 3: Why _____

_____

LEVEL 4: Why _____

_____

LEVEL 5: Why _____

_____

LEVEL 6: Why _____

_____

LEVEL 7: Why _____

_____

My Fear: _____

_____

Do I want this to stop me? _____

_____

My truths: _____

_____

7 Levels Deep OVERCOMING FEAR

The 7 Levels Deep Exercise can be used to help determine what fears are really stopping you, and help weigh the cost and your desire to overcome it.

INSTRUCTIONS: Be completely open and honest with yourself in this exercise. Turn the answer from the previous level into the next question.

MY FEAR DATE: _____

LEVEL 1: What is the fear that is stopping me?

_____

LEVEL 2: Why _____

_____

LEVEL 3: Why _____

_____

LEVEL 4: Why _____

_____

LEVEL 5: Why _____

_____

LEVEL 6: Why _____

_____

LEVEL 7: Why _____

_____

My Fear: _____

_____

Do I want this to stop me? _____

_____

My truths: _____

_____

7 Levels Deep OVERCOMING FEAR

The 7 Levels Deep Exercise can be used to help determine what fears are really stopping you, and help weigh the cost and your desire to overcome it.

INSTRUCTIONS: Be completely open and honest with yourself in this exercise. Turn the answer from the previous level into the next question.

MY FEAR DATE: _____

LEVEL 1: What is the fear that is stopping me?
_____

LEVEL 2: Why _____
_____

LEVEL 3: Why _____
_____

LEVEL 4: Why _____
_____

LEVEL 5: Why _____
_____

LEVEL 6: Why _____
_____

LEVEL 7: Why _____
_____

My Fear: _____
_____

Do I want this to stop me? _____
_____

My truths: _____
_____

7 Levels Deep OVERCOMING FEAR

The 7 Levels Deep Exercise can be used to help determine what fears are really stopping you, and help weigh the cost and your desire to overcome it.

INSTRUCTIONS: Be completely open and honest with yourself in this exercise. Turn the answer from the previous level into the next question.

MY FEAR DATE: _____

LEVEL 1: What is the fear that is stopping me?

_____

LEVEL 2: Why _____

_____

LEVEL 3: Why _____

_____

LEVEL 4: Why _____

_____

LEVEL 5: Why _____

_____

LEVEL 6: Why _____

_____

LEVEL 7: Why _____

_____

My Fear: _____

_____

Do I want this to stop me? _____

_____

My truths: _____

_____

7 Levels Deep OVERCOMING FEAR

The 7 Levels Deep Exercise can be used to help determine what fears are really stopping you, and help weigh the cost and your desire to overcome it.

INSTRUCTIONS: Be completely open and honest with yourself in this exercise. Turn the answer from the previous level into the next question.

MY FEAR   DATE: _____

LEVEL 1: What is the fear that is stopping me?

_____

LEVEL 2: Why _____

_____

LEVEL 3: Why _____

_____

LEVEL 4: Why _____

_____

LEVEL 5: Why _____

_____

LEVEL 6: Why _____

_____

LEVEL 7: Why _____

_____

My Fear: _____

_____

Do I want this to stop me? _____

_____

My truths: _____

_____

7 Levels Deep OVERCOMING FEAR

The 7 Levels Deep Exercise can be used to help determine what fears are really stopping you, and help weigh the cost and your desire to overcome it.

INSTRUCTIONS: Be completely open and honest with yourself in this exercise. Turn the answer from the previous level into the next question.

MY FEAR   DATE: _____

LEVEL 1: What is the fear that is stopping me?

_____

LEVEL 2: Why _____

_____

LEVEL 3: Why _____

_____

LEVEL 4: Why _____

_____

LEVEL 5: Why _____

_____

LEVEL 6: Why _____

_____

LEVEL 7: Why _____

_____

My Fear: _____

_____

Do I want this to stop me? _____

_____

My truths: _____

_____

7 Levels Deep OVERCOMING FEAR

The 7 Levels Deep Exercise can be used to help determine what fears are really stopping you, and help weigh the cost and your desire to overcome it.

INSTRUCTIONS: Be completely open and honest with yourself in this exercise. Turn the answer from the previous level into the next question.

MY FEAR   DATE: _____

LEVEL 1: What is the fear that is stopping me?

_____

LEVEL 2: Why _____

_____

LEVEL 3: Why _____

_____

LEVEL 4: Why _____

_____

LEVEL 5: Why _____

_____

LEVEL 6: Why _____

_____

LEVEL 7: Why _____

_____

My Fear: _____

_____

Do I want this to stop me? _____

_____

My truths: _____

_____

7 Levels Deep OVERCOMING FEAR

The 7 Levels Deep Exercise can be used to help determine what fears are really stopping you, and help weigh the cost and your desire to overcome it.

INSTRUCTIONS: Be completely open and honest with yourself in this exercise. Turn the answer from the previous level into the next question.

MY FEAR   DATE: _____

LEVEL 1: What is the fear that is stopping me?

_____

LEVEL 2: Why _____

_____

LEVEL 3: Why _____

_____

LEVEL 4: Why _____

_____

LEVEL 5: Why _____

_____

LEVEL 6: Why _____

_____

LEVEL 7: Why _____

_____

My Fear: _____

_____

Do I want this to stop me? _____

_____

My truths: _____

_____

7 Levels Deep OVERCOMING FEAR

The 7 Levels Deep Exercise can be used to help determine what fears are really stopping you, and help weigh the cost and your desire to overcome it.

INSTRUCTIONS: Be completely open and honest with yourself in this exercise. Turn the answer from the previous level into the next question.

MY FEAR   DATE: _____

LEVEL 1: What is the fear that is stopping me?

_____

LEVEL 2: Why _____

_____

LEVEL 3: Why _____

_____

LEVEL 4: Why _____

_____

LEVEL 5: Why _____

_____

LEVEL 6: Why _____

_____

LEVEL 7: Why _____

_____

My Fear: _____

_____

Do I want this to stop me? _____

_____

My truths: _____

_____

7 Levels Deep OVERCOMING FEAR

The 7 Levels Deep Exercise can be used to help determine what fears are really stopping you, and help weigh the cost and your desire to overcome it.

INSTRUCTIONS: Be completely open and honest with yourself in this exercise. Turn the answer from the previous level into the next question.

MY FEAR   DATE: _____

LEVEL 1: What is the fear that is stopping me?

_____

LEVEL 2: Why _____

_____

LEVEL 3: Why _____

_____

LEVEL 4: Why _____

_____

LEVEL 5: Why _____

_____

LEVEL 6: Why _____

_____

LEVEL 7: Why _____

_____

My Fear: _____

_____

Do I want this to stop me? _____

_____

My truths: _____

_____

7 Levels Deep OVERCOMING FEAR

The 7 Levels Deep Exercise can be used to help determine what fears are really stopping you, and help weigh the cost and your desire to overcome it.

INSTRUCTIONS: Be completely open and honest with yourself in this exercise. Turn the answer from the previous level into the next question.

MY FEAR DATE: _____

LEVEL 1: What is the fear that is stopping me?

_____

LEVEL 2: Why _____

_____

LEVEL 3: Why _____

_____

LEVEL 4: Why _____

_____

LEVEL 5: Why _____

_____

LEVEL 6: Why _____

_____

LEVEL 7: Why _____

_____

My Fear: _____

_____

Do I want this to stop me? _____

_____

My truths: _____

_____

But seek ye FIRST *the kingdom of God, and his righteousness; and* ALL THESE THINGS *shall be added unto you.*

MATTHEW 6:33

BELIEVE YE *that I am able to do this? They said unto him, Yea, Lord…* ACCORDING TO YOUR FAITH *be it unto you.*

MATTHEW 9:28-29

GOAL SETTING
Worksheets

WORKSHEET INSTRUCTIONS

The following worksheets will help you move through your goals in three-month increments. Big goals often take at least a quarter of the year to complete. So, you can break your larger goal down into four smaller goals, or you can work on four separate goals. If you ask and listen, you will be inspired by God.

In the following worksheets you will find:

- **15 Weekly Goal sheets each quarter.** I share five weekly sheets per month because some months have 4 weeks and others overlap into five. Skip week five if you have a month with only four weeks. The weekly goal section includes:
    - Mini-goals
    - Obstacles
    - End of Week Summary
    - Notes, Ideas or Journaling

- **These same worksheets will repeat for each quarter.**

- **4 End of the Month Summary sheets** (Use these to record your accomplishments for the month)

- **End of Quarter Summary sheets** (Use these to record your accomplishments for the quarter)

- At the end of the year, you will have one page for your **End of the Year Summary**

You don't have to start in January. Start today where you are and move forward in weekly increments until you have achieved your goal.

FIRST QUARTER
Goal Worksheets

GOALS: WEEK ___

Trust in the Lord, and do good.

PSALM 37:3

My Inspired Resolution: DATE: _____

_____

MINI-GOALS – What I will accomplish this week + reward for each goal:

_____

_____

_____

_____

Now, **talk to God about it**. Tell Him about your weekly goals and ask for courage, faith, and patience to accomplish them.

Begin each morning with prayer. Tell God about your mini-goals and ask for the wisdom and determination to accomplish them. Schedule how you will work on one of your mini-goals that day and do it! Meditate and envision yourself accomplishing each goal and enjoying your reward.

Don't be discouraged if life throws curve balls at you during the day. Life happens. Give yourself grace and keep going. Learn more about how to overcome obstacles on the next page.

End every day with a prayer of thanks and a report of how you have done with your goals that day.

List any additional ideas or thoughts after your prayers below.

_____

_____

_____

Be flexible enough to incorporate additional ideas into your weekly goals. This is how you learn to trust God and be spontaneous enough to walk through doors that come up mid-week.

OBSTACLES: WEEK __

For this thing I besought the Lord thrice, that it might depart from me.

2 CORINTHIANS 12:8

During the week, take a few moments to evaluate this question:

What obstacles am I facing? _____

_____
_____
_____
_____

Talk to God at night about these obstacles and ask for His help. Turning it over to God doesn't mean you do nothing, but that you don't need to stress or worry. With God as your partner, you know you just need to do what you are able to do and leave the rest in His hands.

I have had some amazing experiences going to sleep with an obstacle or question and then waking at 4:30am with the answer. I know that between God and our subconscious working on the problem, ideas will come.

When you awake the next morning, before you look at any device, spend time thinking about your obstacle. Keep a prayer in your heart throughout the day and ask God to help you see or hear the solution. Write down any additional ideas or impressions below that may come to you. Then tweak it or find someone who can help you.

_____
_____
_____
_____
_____

Keep working and moving forward. If you find a closed door, trust that God has a better door for you to walk toward and keep your momentum going. You can also shift your focus to another mini goal until you the way opens. Pray and God will guide you.

END OF WEEK SUMMARY: WEEK __

But SEEK YE FIRST THE KINGDOM OF GOD, *and his righteousness; and all these things shall be added unto you.*

MATTHEW 6:33

God knows you and your situation perfectly. Remember the principle of grace as you review your week, and don't be hard on yourself.

What mini-goals did I accomplish this week?

_____
_____
_____
_____

What rewards did I enjoy?

_____
_____
_____
_____

What other things did I accomplish this week?

_____
_____
_____
_____

Are there any mini-goals that need to be modified or carried over to next week?

_____
_____
_____
_____

MY MIRACLES: Obstacles I have overcome this week and other ways I have seen God's hand.

Obstacles I have *"given to God"* for further illumination:

NOTES:

GOALS: WEEK __

I can do all things through Christ which strengtheneth me.

PHILIPPIANS 4:13

My Inspired Resolution: DATE: _____

_____

MINI-GOALS – What I will accomplish this week + reward for each goal:

_____
_____
_____
_____

Now, **talk to God about it**. Tell Him about your weekly goals and ask for courage, faith, and patience to accomplish them.

Begin each morning with prayer. Tell God about your mini-goals and ask for the wisdom and determination to accomplish them. Schedule how you will work on one of your mini-goals that day and do it! Meditate and envision yourself accomplishing each goal and enjoying your reward.

Don't be discouraged if life throws curve balls at you during the day. Life happens. Give yourself grace and keep going. Learn more about how to overcome obstacles on the next page.

End every day with a prayer of thanks and a report of how you have done with your goals that day.

List any additional ideas or thoughts after your prayers below.

_____
_____
_____
_____

Be flexible enough to incorporate additional ideas into your weekly goals. This is how you learn to trust God and be spontaneous enough to walk through doors that come up mid-week.

OBSTACLES: WEEK __

We glory in tribulations also: knowing that tribulation worketh patience.

ROMANS 5:3

During the week, take a few moments to evaluate this question:

What obstacles am I facing? _____

_____

_____

_____

_____

Talk to God at night about these obstacles and ask for His help. Turning it over to God doesn't mean you do nothing, but that you don't need to stress or worry. With God as your partner, you know you just need to do what you are able to do and leave the rest in His hands.

I have had some amazing experiences going to sleep with an obstacle or question and then waking at 4:30am with the answer. I know that between God and our subconscious working on the problem, ideas will come.

When you awake the next morning, before you look at any device, spend time thinking about your obstacle. Keep a prayer in your heart throughout the day and ask God to help you see or hear the solution. Write down any additional ideas or impressions below that may come to you. Then tweak it or find someone who can help you.

_____

_____

_____

_____

_____

Keep working and moving forward. If you find a closed door, trust that God has a better door for you to walk toward and keep your momentum going. You can also shift your focus to another mini goal until you the way opens. Pray and God will guide you.

END OF WEEK SUMMARY: WEEK __

Know ye not that they which run in a race run all, but one receiveth the prize? So run, that ye may obtain.

1 CORINTHIANS 9:24

God knows you and your situation perfectly. Remember the principle of grace as you review your week, and don't be hard on yourself.

What mini-goals did I accomplish this week?

___

What rewards did I enjoy?

___

What other things did I accomplish this week?

___

Are there any mini-goals that need to be modified or carried over to next week?

___

MY MIRACLES: Obstacles I have overcome this week and other ways I have seen God's hand.

Obstacles I have *"given to God"* for further illumination:

NOTES:

GOALS: WEEK ___

All that the Lord hath said will we do.

EXODUS 24:7

My Inspired Resolution: DATE: _____

MINI-GOALS – What I will accomplish this week + reward for each goal:

Now, **talk to God about it**. Tell Him about your weekly goals and ask for courage, faith, and patience to accomplish them.

Begin each morning with prayer. Tell God about your mini-goals and ask for the wisdom and determination to accomplish them. Schedule how you will work on one of your mini-goals that day and do it! Meditate and envision yourself accomplishing each goal and enjoying your reward.

Don't be discouraged if life throws curve balls at you during the day. Life happens. Give yourself grace and keep going. Learn more about how to overcome obstacles on the next page.

End every day with a prayer of thanks and a report of how you have done with your goals that day.

List any additional ideas or thoughts after your prayers below.

Be flexible enough to incorporate additional ideas into your weekly goals. This is how you learn to trust God and be spontaneous enough to walk through doors that come up mid-week.

OBSTACLES: WEEK __

If ye have faith as a grain of mustard seed, ye shall say unto this mountain, Remove hence to yonder place; and it shall remove; and nothing shall be impossible unto you.

MATTHEW 17:20

During the week, take a few moments to evaluate this question:

What obstacles am I facing? _____

_____
_____
_____
_____

Talk to God at night about these obstacles and ask for His help. Turning it over to God doesn't mean you do nothing, but that you don't need to stress or worry. With God as your partner, you know you just need to do what you are able to do and leave the rest in His hands.

I have had some amazing experiences going to sleep with an obstacle or question and then waking at 4:30am with the answer. I know that between God and our subconscious working on the problem, ideas will come.

When you awake the next morning, before you look at any device, spend time thinking about your obstacle. Keep a prayer in your heart throughout the day and ask God to help you see or hear the solution. Write down any additional ideas or impressions below that may come to you. Then tweak it or find someone who can help you.

_____
_____
_____
_____

Keep working and moving forward. If you find a closed door, trust that God has a better door for you to walk toward and keep your momentum going. You can also shift your focus to another mini goal until you the way opens. Pray and God will guide you.

END OF WEEK SUMMARY: WEEK __

Fear thou not; for I am with thee: be not dismayed; for I am thy God: I will strengthen thee; yea, I will help thee; yea, I will uphold thee with the right hand of my righteousness.

ISAIAH 41:10

God knows you and your situation perfectly. Remember the principle of grace as you review your week, and don't be hard on yourself.

What mini-goals did I accomplish this week?

_____
_____
_____
_____

What rewards did I enjoy?

_____
_____
_____
_____

What other things did I accomplish this week?

_____
_____
_____
_____

Are there any mini-goals that need to be modified or carried over to next week?

_____
_____
_____

MY MIRACLES: Obstacles I have overcome this week and other ways I have seen God's hand.

Obstacles I have *"given to God"* for further illumination:

NOTES:

GOALS: WEEK ___

Trust in the Lord with all thine heart; and lean not unto thine own understanding. In all thy ways acknowledge Him, and He shall direct thy paths.

PROVERBS 3:5-6

My Inspired Resolution: DATE: _____

_____

MINI-GOALS – What I will accomplish this week + reward for each goal:

_____
_____
_____
_____

Now, **talk to God about it**. Tell Him about your weekly goals and ask for courage, faith, and patience to accomplish them.

Begin each morning with prayer. Tell God about your mini-goals and ask for the wisdom and determination to accomplish them. Schedule how you will work on one of your mini-goals that day and do it! Meditate and envision yourself accomplishing each goal and enjoying your reward.

Don't be discouraged if life throws curve balls at you during the day. Life happens. Give yourself grace and keep going. Learn more about how to overcome obstacles on the next page.

End every day with a prayer of thanks and a report of how you have done with your goals that day.

List any additional ideas or thoughts after your prayers below.

_____
_____
_____
_____

Be flexible enough to incorporate additional ideas into your weekly goals. This is how you learn to trust God and be spontaneous enough to walk through doors that come up mid-week.

OBSTACLES: WEEK __

Prepare the way, take up the stumblingblock out of the way of my people.

ISAIAH 57:14

During the week, take a few moments to evaluate this question:

What obstacles am I facing? _____

_____
_____
_____
_____

Talk to God at night about these obstacles and ask for His help. Turning it over to God doesn't mean you do nothing, but that you don't need to stress or worry. With God as your partner, you know you just need to do what you are able to do and leave the rest in His hands.

I have had some amazing experiences going to sleep with an obstacle or question and then waking at 4:30am with the answer. I know that between God and our subconscious working on the problem, ideas will come.

When you awake the next morning, before you look at any device, spend time thinking about your obstacle. Keep a prayer in your heart throughout the day and ask God to help you see or hear the solution. Write down any additional ideas or impressions below that may come to you. Then tweak it or find someone who can help you.

_____
_____
_____
_____
_____

Keep working and moving forward. If you find a closed door, trust that God has a better door for you to walk toward and keep your momentum going. You can also shift your focus to another mini goal until you the way opens. Pray and God will guide you.

END OF WEEK SUMMARY: WEEK ___

Commit thy works unto the Lord, and thy thoughts shall be established.

PROVERBS 16:3

God knows you and your situation perfectly. Remember the principle of grace as you review your week, and don't be hard on yourself.

What mini-goals did I accomplish this week?

_____
_____
_____
_____

What rewards did I enjoy?

_____
_____
_____
_____

What other things did I accomplish this week?

_____
_____
_____
_____

Are there any mini-goals that need to be modified or carried over to next week?

_____
_____
_____
_____

MY MIRACLES: Obstacles I have overcome this week and other ways I have seen God's hand.

_____
_____
_____
_____
_____

Obstacles I have *"given to God"* for further illumination:

_____
_____
_____
_____

NOTES: _____

_____
_____
_____
_____
_____
_____
_____
_____
_____
_____
_____
_____

GOALS: WEEK ___

For God hath not given us the spirit of fear; but of power, and of love, and of a sound mind."
2 TIMOTHY 1:7

My Inspired Resolution: DATE: _____

MINI-GOALS – What I will accomplish this week + reward for each goal:

Now, **talk to God about it**. Tell Him about your weekly goals and ask for courage, faith, and patience to accomplish them.

Begin each morning with prayer. Tell God about your mini-goals and ask for the wisdom and determination to accomplish them. Schedule how you will work on one of your mini-goals that day and do it! Meditate and envision yourself accomplishing each goal and enjoying your reward.

Don't be discouraged if life throws curve balls at you during the day. Life happens. Give yourself grace and keep going. Learn more about how to overcome obstacles on the next page.

End every day with a prayer of thanks and a report of how you have done with your goals that day.

List any additional ideas or thoughts after your prayers below.

Be flexible enough to incorporate additional ideas into your weekly goals. This is how you learn to trust God and be spontaneous enough to walk through doors that come up mid-week.

OBSTACLES: WEEK __

The LORD shall fight for you, and ye shall hold your peace.

EXODUS 14:14

During the week, take a few moments to evaluate this question:

What obstacles am I facing? _____

_____

_____

_____

_____

Talk to God at night about these obstacles and ask for His help. Turning it over to God doesn't mean you do nothing, but that you don't need to stress or worry. With God as your partner, you know you just need to do what you are able to do and leave the rest in His hands.

I have had some amazing experiences going to sleep with an obstacle or question and then waking at 4:30am with the answer. I know that between God and our subconscious working on the problem, ideas will come.

When you awake the next morning, before you look at any device, spend time thinking about your obstacle. Keep a prayer in your heart throughout the day and ask God to help you see or hear the solution. Write down any additional ideas or impressions below that may come to you. Then tweak it or find someone who can help you.

_____

_____

_____

_____

_____

Keep working and moving forward. If you find a closed door, trust that God has a better door for you to walk toward and keep your momentum going. You can also shift your focus to another mini goal until you the way opens. Pray and God will guide you.

END OF WEEK SUMMARY: WEEK __

A man's heart deviseth his way: but the Lord directeth his steps.

PROVERBS 16:9

God knows you and your situation perfectly. Remember the principle of grace as you review your week, and don't be hard on yourself.

What mini-goals did I accomplish this week?

_____
_____
_____
_____

What rewards did I enjoy?

_____
_____
_____
_____

What other things did I accomplish this week?

_____
_____
_____
_____

Are there any mini-goals that need to be modified or carried over to next week?

_____
_____
_____
_____

MY MIRACLES: Obstacles I have overcome this week and other ways I have seen God's hand.

_____
_____
_____
_____
_____

Obstacles I have *"given to God"* for further illumination:

_____
_____
_____
_____

NOTES: _____
_____
_____
_____
_____
_____
_____
_____
_____
_____
_____
_____
_____

END OF MONTH SUMMARY

In all thy ways acknowledge him, and he shall direct thy paths.
PROVERBS 3:6

Fill in your data from this month's weekly goal sheets here.

What mini-goals did I accomplish this month?

_____
_____
_____
_____
_____
_____
_____
_____
_____
_____

What rewards did I enjoy?

_____
_____
_____
_____

What other things did I accomplish this month?

_____
_____
_____
_____
_____
_____
_____
_____
_____
_____
_____
_____

MY MIRACLES: Obstacles I have overcome this month and other ways I have seen God's hand:

_____
_____
_____
_____
_____
_____
_____
_____
_____
_____
_____
_____

How have I changed?

_____

What mini-goals do I want to work on next month to keep moving forward?

_____

Will you please email me at **tamarakandersonauthor@gmail.com** to tell me about your accomplishments this month? I'd love to rejoice with you in your success!

NOTES:

GOALS: WEEK ___

Shew me thy ways, O Lord; teach me thy paths.

PSALM 25:4

My Inspired Resolution: DATE: _____

MINI-GOALS – What I will accomplish this week + reward for each goal:

Now, **talk to God about it**. Tell Him about your weekly goals and ask for courage, faith, and patience to accomplish them.

Begin each morning with prayer. Tell God about your mini-goals and ask for the wisdom and determination to accomplish them. Schedule how you will work on one of your mini-goals that day and do it! Meditate and envision yourself accomplishing each goal and enjoying your reward.

Don't be discouraged if life throws curve balls at you during the day. Life happens. Give yourself grace and keep going. Learn more about how to overcome obstacles on the next page.

End every day with a prayer of thanks and a report of how you have done with your goals that day.

List any additional ideas or thoughts after your prayers below.

Be flexible enough to incorporate additional ideas into your weekly goals. This is how you learn to trust God and be spontaneous enough to walk through doors that come up mid-week.

OBSTACLES: WEEK __

In the world ye shall have tribulation: but be of good cheer; I have overcome the world.
JOHN 16:33

During the week, take a few moments to evaluate this question:

What obstacles am I facing? _____

_____
_____
_____
_____

Talk to God at night about these obstacles and ask for His help. Turning it over to God doesn't mean you do nothing, but that you don't need to stress or worry. With God as your partner, you know you just need to do what you are able to do and leave the rest in His hands.

I have had some amazing experiences going to sleep with an obstacle or question and then waking at 4:30am with the answer. I know that between God and our subconscious working on the problem, ideas will come.

When you awake the next morning, before you look at any device, spend time thinking about your obstacle. Keep a prayer in your heart throughout the day and ask God to help you see or hear the solution. Write down any additional ideas or impressions below that may come to you. Then tweak it or find someone who can help you.

_____
_____
_____
_____
_____

Keep working and moving forward. If you find a closed door, trust that God has a better door for you to walk toward and keep your momentum going. You can also shift your focus to another mini goal until you the way opens. Pray and God will guide you.

END OF WEEK SUMMARY: WEEK __

Where there is no vision, the people perish.

PROVERBS 29:18

God knows you and your situation perfectly. Remember the principle of grace as you review your week, and don't be hard on yourself.

What mini-goals did I accomplish this week?

_____
_____
_____
_____

What rewards did I enjoy?

_____
_____
_____
_____

What other things did I accomplish this week?

_____
_____
_____
_____

Are there any mini-goals that need to be modified or carried over to next week?

_____
_____
_____
_____

MY MIRACLES: Obstacles I have overcome this week and other ways I have seen God's hand.

_____
_____
_____
_____
_____

Obstacles I have *"given to God"* for further illumination:

_____
_____
_____
_____

NOTES: _____
_____
_____
_____
_____
_____
_____
_____
_____
_____
_____
_____

GOALS: WEEK __

The Lord is my shepherd. I shall not want... He leadeth me in the paths of righteousness... I will fear no evil: for thou art with me.

PSALM 23: 1, 3, 4

My Inspired Resolution: DATE: _____

MINI-GOALS – What I will accomplish this week + reward for each goal:

Now, **talk to God about it**. Tell Him about your weekly goals and ask for courage, faith, and patience to accomplish them.

Begin each morning with prayer. Tell God about your mini-goals and ask for the wisdom and determination to accomplish them. Schedule how you will work on one of your mini-goals that day and do it! Meditate and envision yourself accomplishing each goal and enjoying your reward.

Don't be discouraged if life throws curve balls at you during the day. Life happens. Give yourself grace and keep going. Learn more about how to overcome obstacles on the next page.

End every day with a prayer of thanks and a report of how you have done with your goals that day.

List any additional ideas or thoughts after your prayers below.

Be flexible enough to incorporate additional ideas into your weekly goals. This is how you learn to trust God and be spontaneous enough to walk through doors that come up mid-week.

OBSTACLES: WEEK __

Be not overcome of evil, but overcome evil with good.

ROMANS 12:21

During the week, take a few moments to evaluate this question:

What obstacles am I facing? _____

_____

_____

_____

_____

Talk to God at night about these obstacles and ask for His help. Turning it over to God doesn't mean you do nothing, but that you don't need to stress or worry. With God as your partner, you know you just need to do what you are able to do and leave the rest in His hands.

I have had some amazing experiences going to sleep with an obstacle or question and then waking at 4:30am with the answer. I know that between God and our subconscious working on the problem, ideas will come.

When you awake the next morning, before you look at any device, spend time thinking about your obstacle. Keep a prayer in your heart throughout the day and ask God to help you see or hear the solution. Write down any additional ideas or impressions below that may come to you. Then tweak it or find someone who can help you.

_____

_____

_____

_____

_____

Keep working and moving forward. If you find a closed door, trust that God has a better door for you to walk toward and keep your momentum going. You can also shift your focus to another mini goal until you the way opens. Pray and God will guide you.

END OF WEEK SUMMARY: WEEK ___

I press toward the mark.

PHILIPPIANS 3:14

God knows you and your situation perfectly. Remember the principle of grace as you review your week, and don't be hard on yourself.

What mini-goals did I accomplish this week?

_____
_____
_____
_____

What rewards did I enjoy?

_____
_____
_____
_____

What other things did I accomplish this week?

_____
_____
_____
_____

Are there any mini-goals that need to be modified or carried over to next week?

_____
_____
_____
_____

MY MIRACLES: Obstacles I have overcome this week and other ways I have seen God's hand.

Obstacles I have *"given to God"* for further illumination:

NOTES:

GOALS: WEEK __

For this God is our God for ever and ever: He will be our guide even unto death.

PSALM 48:14

My Inspired Resolution: DATE: _____

MINI-GOALS – What I will accomplish this week + reward for each goal:

Now, **talk to God about it**. Tell Him about your weekly goals and ask for courage, faith, and patience to accomplish them.

Begin each morning with prayer. Tell God about your mini-goals and ask for the wisdom and determination to accomplish them. Schedule how you will work on one of your mini-goals that day and do it! Meditate and envision yourself accomplishing each goal and enjoying your reward.

Don't be discouraged if life throws curve balls at you during the day. Life happens. Give yourself grace and keep going. Learn more about how to overcome obstacles on the next page.

End every day with a prayer of thanks and a report of how you have done with your goals that day.

List any additional ideas or thoughts after your prayers below.

Be flexible enough to incorporate additional ideas into your weekly goals. This is how you learn to trust God and be spontaneous enough to walk through doors that come up mid-week.

OBSTACLES: WEEK __

Thanks be to God, which giveth us the victory through our Lord Jesus Christ.

1 CORINTHIANS 15:57

During the week, take a few moments to evaluate this question:

What obstacles am I facing? _____

_____

_____

_____

_____

Talk to God at night about these obstacles and ask for His help. Turning it over to God doesn't mean you do nothing, but that you don't need to stress or worry. With God as your partner, you know you just need to do what you are able to do and leave the rest in His hands.

I have had some amazing experiences going to sleep with an obstacle or question and then waking at 4:30am with the answer. I know that between God and our subconscious working on the problem, ideas will come.

When you awake the next morning, before you look at any device, spend time thinking about your obstacle. Keep a prayer in your heart throughout the day and ask God to help you see or hear the solution. Write down any additional ideas or impressions below that may come to you. Then tweak it or find someone who can help you.

_____

_____

_____

_____

_____

Keep working and moving forward. If you find a closed door, trust that God has a better door for you to walk toward and keep your momentum going. You can also shift your focus to another mini goal until you the way opens. Pray and God will guide you.

END OF WEEK SUMMARY: WEEK __

Commit thy way unto the LORD; trust also in him; and he shall bring it to pass.

PSALM 37:5

God knows you and your situation perfectly. Remember the principle of grace as you review your week, and don't be hard on yourself.

What mini-goals did I accomplish this week?

___

What rewards did I enjoy?

___

What other things did I accomplish this week?

___

Are there any mini-goals that need to be modified or carried over to next week?

___

MY MIRACLES: Obstacles I have overcome this week and other ways I have seen God's hand.

_____
_____
_____
_____
_____

Obstacles I have *"given to God"* for further illumination:

_____
_____
_____
_____

NOTES: _____

_____
_____
_____
_____
_____
_____
_____
_____
_____
_____
_____

GOALS: WEEK ___

For thou art my rock and my fortress;
therefore for thy name's sake lead me, and guide me.

PSALM 31:3

My Inspired Resolution: DATE: _____

_____

MINI-GOALS – What I will accomplish this week + reward for each goal:

_____

_____

_____

_____

Now, **talk to God about it**. Tell Him about your weekly goals and ask for courage, faith, and patience to accomplish them.

Begin each morning with prayer. Tell God about your mini-goals and ask for the wisdom and determination to accomplish them. Schedule how you will work on one of your mini-goals that day and do it! Meditate and envision yourself accomplishing each goal and enjoying your reward.

Don't be discouraged if life throws curve balls at you during the day. Life happens. Give yourself grace and keep going. Learn more about how to overcome obstacles on the next page.

End every day with a prayer of thanks and a report of how you have done with your goals that day.

List any additional ideas or thoughts after your prayers below.

_____

_____

_____

Be flexible enough to incorporate additional ideas into your weekly goals. This is how you learn to trust God and be spontaneous enough to walk through doors that come up mid-week.

OBSTACLES: WEEK __

In all these things we are more than conquerors through him that loved us.

ROMANS 8:37

During the week, take a few moments to evaluate this question:

What obstacles am I facing? _____

_____

_____

_____

_____

Talk to God at night about these obstacles and ask for His help. Turning it over to God doesn't mean you do nothing, but that you don't need to stress or worry. With God as your partner, you know you just need to do what you are able to do and leave the rest in His hands.

I have had some amazing experiences going to sleep with an obstacle or question and then waking at 4:30am with the answer. I know that between God and our subconscious working on the problem, ideas will come.

When you awake the next morning, before you look at any device, spend time thinking about your obstacle. Keep a prayer in your heart throughout the day and ask God to help you see or hear the solution. Write down any additional ideas or impressions below that may come to you. Then tweak it or find someone who can help you.

_____

_____

_____

_____

_____

Keep working and moving forward. If you find a closed door, trust that God has a better door for you to walk toward and keep your momentum going. You can also shift your focus to another mini goal until you the way opens. Pray and God will guide you.

END OF WEEK SUMMARY: WEEK __

Be ye strong therefore, and let not your hands be weak: for your work shall be rewarded.

2 CHRONICLES 15:7

God knows you and your situation perfectly. Remember the principle of grace as you review your week, and don't be hard on yourself.

What mini-goals did I accomplish this week?

_____
_____
_____
_____

What rewards did I enjoy?

_____
_____
_____
_____

What other things did I accomplish this week?

_____
_____
_____
_____

Are there any mini-goals that need to be modified or carried over to next week?

_____
_____
_____
_____

MY MIRACLES: Obstacles I have overcome this week and other ways I have seen God's hand.

_____
_____
_____
_____
_____

Obstacles I have *"given to God"* for further illumination:

_____
_____
_____
_____

NOTES: _____
_____
_____
_____
_____
_____
_____
_____
_____
_____
_____
_____
_____
_____

GOALS: WEEK __

Guide our feet into the way of peace.

LUKE 1:79

My Inspired Resolution: DATE: _____

MINI-GOALS − What I will accomplish this week + reward for each goal:

Now, **talk to God about it**. Tell Him about your weekly goals and ask for courage, faith, and patience to accomplish them.

Begin each morning with prayer. Tell God about your mini-goals and ask for the wisdom and determination to accomplish them. Schedule how you will work on one of your mini-goals that day and do it! Meditate and envision yourself accomplishing each goal and enjoying your reward.

Don't be discouraged if life throws curve balls at you during the day. Life happens. Give yourself grace and keep going. Learn more about how to overcome obstacles on the next page.

End every day with a prayer of thanks and a report of how you have done with your goals that day.

List any additional ideas or thoughts after your prayers below.

Be flexible enough to incorporate additional ideas into your weekly goals. This is how you learn to trust God and be spontaneous enough to walk through doors that come up mid-week.

OBSTACLES: WEEK __

Let us run with patience the race that is set before us.

HEBREWS 12:1

During the week, take a few moments to evaluate this question:

What obstacles am I facing? _____

_____
_____
_____
_____

Talk to God at night about these obstacles and ask for His help. Turning it over to God doesn't mean you do nothing, but that you don't need to stress or worry. With God as your partner, you know you just need to do what you are able to do and leave the rest in His hands.

I have had some amazing experiences going to sleep with an obstacle or question and then waking at 4:30am with the answer. I know that between God and our subconscious working on the problem, ideas will come.

When you awake the next morning, before you look at any device, spend time thinking about your obstacle. Keep a prayer in your heart throughout the day and ask God to help you see or hear the solution. Write down any additional ideas or impressions below that may come to you. Then tweak it or find someone who can help you.

_____
_____
_____
_____
_____
_____

Keep working and moving forward. If you find a closed door, trust that God has a better door for you to walk toward and keep your momentum going. You can also shift your focus to another mini goal until you the way opens. Pray and God will guide you.

END OF WEEK SUMMARY: WEEK __

Delight thyself also in the LORD; and he shall give thee the desires of thine heart.

PSALM 37:4

God knows you and your situation perfectly. Remember the principle of grace as you review your week, and don't be hard on yourself.

What mini-goals did I accomplish this week?

_____
_____
_____
_____

What rewards did I enjoy?

_____
_____
_____
_____

What other things did I accomplish this week?

_____
_____
_____
_____

Are there any mini-goals that need to be modified or carried over to next week?

_____
_____
_____
_____

MY MIRACLES: Obstacles I have overcome this week and other ways I have seen God's hand.

_____
_____
_____
_____
_____
_____

Obstacles I have *"given to God"* for further illumination:

_____
_____
_____
_____

NOTES: _____
_____
_____
_____
_____
_____
_____
_____
_____
_____
_____
_____
_____

END OF MONTH SUMMARY

Cast not away therefore your confidence, ... For ye have need of patience, that, after ye have done the will of God, ye might receive the promise

HEBREWS 10:35-36

Fill in your data from this month's weekly goal sheets here.

What mini-goals did I accomplish this month?

_____
_____
_____
_____
_____
_____
_____
_____
_____
_____

What rewards did I enjoy?

_____
_____
_____
_____
_____

What other things did I accomplish this month?

MY MIRACLES: Obstacles I have overcome this month and other ways I have seen God's hand:

How have I changed?

_____

What mini-goals do I want to work on next month to keep moving forward?

_____

Will you please email me at **tamarakandersonauthor@gmail.com** to tell me about your accomplishments this month? I'd love to rejoice with you in your success!

NOTES:

GOALS: WEEK ___

*I will instruct thee and teach thee in the way which thou shalt go:
I will guide thee with mine eye.*

PSALM 32:8

My Inspired Resolution: DATE: _____

_____

MINI-GOALS – What I will accomplish this week + reward for each goal:

_____

_____

_____

Now, **talk to God about it**. Tell Him about your weekly goals and ask for courage, faith, and patience to accomplish them.

Begin each morning with prayer. Tell God about your mini-goals and ask for the wisdom and determination to accomplish them. Schedule how you will work on one of your mini-goals that day and do it! Meditate and envision yourself accomplishing each goal and enjoying your reward.

Don't be discouraged if life throws curve balls at you during the day. Life happens. Give yourself grace and keep going. Learn more about how to overcome obstacles on the next page.

End every day with a prayer of thanks and a report of how you have done with your goals that day.

List any additional ideas or thoughts after your prayers below.

_____

_____

_____

Be flexible enough to incorporate additional ideas into your weekly goals. This is how you learn to trust God and be spontaneous enough to walk through doors that come up mid-week.

OBSTACLES: WEEK __

Fight the good fight of faith.

1 TIMOTHY 6:12

During the week, take a few moments to evaluate this question:

What obstacles am I facing? _____

_____

_____

_____

Talk to God at night about these obstacles and ask for His help. Turning it over to God doesn't mean you do nothing, but that you don't need to stress or worry. With God as your partner, you know you just need to do what you are able to do and leave the rest in His hands.

I have had some amazing experiences going to sleep with an obstacle or question and then waking at 4:30am with the answer. I know that between God and our subconscious working on the problem, ideas will come.

When you awake the next morning, before you look at any device, spend time thinking about your obstacle. Keep a prayer in your heart throughout the day and ask God to help you see or hear the solution. Write down any additional ideas or impressions below that may come to you. Then tweak it or find someone who can help you.

_____

_____

_____

_____

Keep working and moving forward. If you find a closed door, trust that God has a better door for you to walk toward and keep your momentum going. You can also shift your focus to another mini goal until you the way opens. Pray and God will guide you.

END OF WEEK SUMMARY: WEEK __

But Jesus beheld them, and said unto them,
With men this is impossible; but with God all things are possible.

MATTHEW 19:26

God knows you and your situation perfectly. Remember the principle of grace as you review your week, and don't be hard on yourself.

What mini-goals did I accomplish this week?

_____
_____
_____

What rewards did I enjoy?

_____
_____
_____

What other things did I accomplish this week?

_____
_____
_____

Are there any mini-goals that need to be modified or carried over to next week?

_____
_____
_____

MY MIRACLES: Obstacles I have overcome this week and other ways I have seen God's hand.

_____
_____
_____
_____
_____

Obstacles I have *"given to God"* for further illumination:

_____
_____
_____
_____

NOTES: _____
_____
_____
_____
_____
_____
_____
_____
_____
_____
_____
_____

GOALS: WEEK ___

And we know that all things work together for good to them that love God, to them who are the called according to his purpose.

ROMANS 8:28

My Inspired Resolution: DATE: _____

MINI-GOALS – What I will accomplish this week + reward for each goal:

Now, **talk to God about it**. Tell Him about your weekly goals and ask for courage, faith, and patience to accomplish them.

Begin each morning with prayer. Tell God about your mini-goals and ask for the wisdom and determination to accomplish them. Schedule how you will work on one of your mini-goals that day and do it! Meditate and envision yourself accomplishing each goal and enjoying your reward.

Don't be discouraged if life throws curve balls at you during the day. Life happens. Give yourself grace and keep going. Learn more about how to overcome obstacles on the next page.

End every day with a prayer of thanks and a report of how you have done with your goals that day.

List any additional ideas or thoughts after your prayers below.

Be flexible enough to incorporate additional ideas into your weekly goals. This is how you learn to trust God and be spontaneous enough to walk through doors that come up mid-week.

OBSTACLES: WEEK __

Ye are of God, little children, and have overcome them:
because greater is he that is in you, than he that is in the world.

1 JOHN 4:4

During the week, take a few moments to evaluate this question:

What obstacles am I facing? _____
_____
_____
_____
_____

Talk to God at night about these obstacles and ask for His help. Turning it over to God doesn't mean you do nothing, but that you don't need to stress or worry. With God as your partner, you know you just need to do what you are able to do and leave the rest in His hands.

I have had some amazing experiences going to sleep with an obstacle or question and then waking at 4:30am with the answer. I know that between God and our subconscious working on the problem, ideas will come.

When you awake the next morning, before you look at any device, spend time thinking about your obstacle. Keep a prayer in your heart throughout the day and ask God to help you see or hear the solution. Write down any additional ideas or impressions below that may come to you. Then tweak it or find someone who can help you.

_____
_____
_____
_____
_____
_____

Keep working and moving forward. If you find a closed door, trust that God has a better door for you to walk toward and keep your momentum going. You can also shift your focus to another mini goal until you the way opens. Pray and God will guide you.

END OF WEEK SUMMARY: WEEK __

Be ye transformed by the renewing of your mind, that ye may prove what is that good, and acceptable, and perfect, will of God.

ROMANS 12:2

God knows you and your situation perfectly. Remember the principle of grace as you review your week, and don't be hard on yourself.

What mini-goals did I accomplish this week?

_____
_____
_____
_____

What rewards did I enjoy?

_____
_____
_____
_____

What other things did I accomplish this week?

_____
_____
_____
_____

Are there any mini-goals that need to be modified or carried over to next week?

_____
_____
_____

MY MIRACLES: Obstacles I have overcome this week and other ways I have seen God's hand.

Obstacles I have *"given to God"* for further illumination:

NOTES:

GOALS: WEEK ___

But they that wait upon the Lord shall renew their strength; they shall mount up with wings as eagles; they shall run, and not be weary; and they shall walk, and not faint.

ISAIAH 40:31

My Inspired Resolution: DATE: _____

MINI-GOALS – What I will accomplish this week + reward for each goal:

_____

_____

_____

_____

Now, **talk to God about it**. Tell Him about your weekly goals and ask for courage, faith, and patience to accomplish them.

Begin each morning with prayer. Tell God about your mini-goals and ask for the wisdom and determination to accomplish them. Schedule how you will work on one of your mini-goals that day and do it! Meditate and envision yourself accomplishing each goal and enjoying your reward.

Don't be discouraged if life throws curve balls at you during the day. Life happens. Give yourself grace and keep going. Learn more about how to overcome obstacles on the next page.

End every day with a prayer of thanks and a report of how you have done with your goals that day.

List any additional ideas or thoughts after your prayers below.

_____

_____

_____

_____

Be flexible enough to incorporate additional ideas into your weekly goals. This is how you learn to trust God and be spontaneous enough to walk through doors that come up mid-week.

OBSTACLES: WEEK __

O Lord, I beseech thee, send now prosperity.

PSALM 118:25

During the week, take a few moments to evaluate this question:

What obstacles am I facing? _____

_____

_____

_____

_____

Talk to God at night about these obstacles and ask for His help. Turning it over to God doesn't mean you do nothing, but that you don't need to stress or worry. With God as your partner, you know you just need to do what you are able to do and leave the rest in His hands.

I have had some amazing experiences going to sleep with an obstacle or question and then waking at 4:30am with the answer. I know that between God and our subconscious working on the problem, ideas will come.

When you awake the next morning, before you look at any device, spend time thinking about your obstacle. Keep a prayer in your heart throughout the day and ask God to help you see or hear the solution. Write down any additional ideas or impressions below that may come to you. Then tweak it or find someone who can help you.

_____

_____

_____

_____

_____

Keep working and moving forward. If you find a closed door, trust that God has a better door for you to walk toward and keep your momentum going. You can also shift your focus to another mini goal until you the way opens. Pray and God will guide you.

END OF WEEK SUMMARY: WEEK __

Whatsoever things are true, … honest, … just, … pure, … lovely, … good report; if there be any virtue, and if there be any praise, think on these things.

PHILIPPIANS 4:8

God knows you and your situation perfectly. Remember the principle of grace as you review your week, and don't be hard on yourself.

What mini-goals did I accomplish this week?

_____

_____

_____

_____

What rewards did I enjoy?

_____

_____

_____

_____

What other things did I accomplish this week?

_____

_____

_____

_____

Are there any mini-goals that need to be modified or carried over to next week?

_____

_____

_____

MY MIRACLES: Obstacles I have overcome this week and other ways I have seen God's hand.

_____
_____
_____
_____
_____

Obstacles I have *"given to God"* for further illumination:

_____
_____
_____
_____

NOTES: _____
_____
_____
_____
_____
_____
_____
_____
_____
_____
_____
_____
_____

GOALS: WEEK __

Great is thy faithfulness. The Lord is my portion, saith my soul; therefore I will hope in him.
LAMENTATIONS 3:23-24

My Inspired Resolution: DATE: _____

MINI-GOALS – What I will accomplish this week + reward for each goal:

Now, **talk to God about it**. Tell Him about your weekly goals and ask for courage, faith, and patience to accomplish them.

Begin each morning with prayer. Tell God about your mini-goals and ask for the wisdom and determination to accomplish them. Schedule how you will work on one of your mini-goals that day and do it! Meditate and envision yourself accomplishing each goal and enjoying your reward.

Don't be discouraged if life throws curve balls at you during the day. Life happens. Give yourself grace and keep going. Learn more about how to overcome obstacles on the next page.

End every day with a prayer of thanks and a report of how you have done with your goals that day.

List any additional ideas or thoughts after your prayers below.

Be flexible enough to incorporate additional ideas into your weekly goals. This is how you learn to trust God and be spontaneous enough to walk through doors that come up mid-week.

OBSTACLES: WEEK __

Thou shalt preserve me from trouble; thou shalt compass me about with songs of deliverance.

PSALM 32:7

During the week, take a few moments to evaluate this question:

What obstacles am I facing? _____

_____
_____
_____
_____

Talk to God at night about these obstacles and ask for His help. Turning it over to God doesn't mean you do nothing, but that you don't need to stress or worry. With God as your partner, you know you just need to do what you are able to do and leave the rest in His hands.

I have had some amazing experiences going to sleep with an obstacle or question and then waking at 4:30am with the answer. I know that between God and our subconscious working on the problem, ideas will come.

When you awake the next morning, before you look at any device, spend time thinking about your obstacle. Keep a prayer in your heart throughout the day and ask God to help you see or hear the solution. Write down any additional ideas or impressions below that may come to you. Then tweak it or find someone who can help you.

_____
_____
_____
_____
_____

Keep working and moving forward. If you find a closed door, trust that God has a better door for you to walk toward and keep your momentum going. You can also shift your focus to another mini goal until you the way opens. Pray and God will guide you.

END OF WEEK SUMMARY: WEEK __

Jesus saith unto them, My meat is to do the will of him that sent me, and to finish his work.

JOHN 4:34

God knows you and your situation perfectly. Remember the principle of grace as you review your week, and don't be hard on yourself.

What mini-goals did I accomplish this week?

_____
_____
_____
_____

What rewards did I enjoy?

_____
_____
_____
_____

What other things did I accomplish this week?

_____
_____
_____
_____

Are there any mini-goals that need to be modified or carried over to next week?

_____
_____
_____
_____

MY MIRACLES: Obstacles I have overcome this week and other ways I have seen God's hand.

_____
_____
_____
_____
_____

Obstacles I have *"given to God"* for further illumination:

_____
_____
_____
_____

NOTES: _____
_____
_____
_____
_____
_____
_____
_____
_____
_____
_____
_____
_____

GOALS: WEEK __

It is good that a man should both hope and quietly wait for the salvation of the Lord.
LAMENTATIONS 3:26

My Inspired Resolution: DATE: _____

_____

MINI-GOALS – What I will accomplish this week + reward for each goal:

_____
_____
_____
_____

Now, **talk to God about it**. Tell Him about your weekly goals and ask for courage, faith, and patience to accomplish them.

Begin each morning with prayer. Tell God about your mini-goals and ask for the wisdom and determination to accomplish them. Schedule how you will work on one of your mini-goals that day and do it! Meditate and envision yourself accomplishing each goal and enjoying your reward.

Don't be discouraged if life throws curve balls at you during the day. Life happens. Give yourself grace and keep going. Learn more about how to overcome obstacles on the next page.

End every day with a prayer of thanks and a report of how you have done with your goals that day.

List any additional ideas or thoughts after your prayers below.

_____
_____
_____
_____

Be flexible enough to incorporate additional ideas into your weekly goals. This is how you learn to trust God and be spontaneous enough to walk through doors that come up mid-week.

OBSTACLES: WEEK __

And ye shall seek me, and find me, when ye shall search for me with all your heart.

JEREMIAH 29:13

During the week, take a few moments to evaluate this question:

What obstacles am I facing? _____

_____
_____
_____
_____

Talk to God at night about these obstacles and ask for His help. Turning it over to God doesn't mean you do nothing, but that you don't need to stress or worry. With God as your partner, you know you just need to do what you are able to do and leave the rest in His hands.

I have had some amazing experiences going to sleep with an obstacle or question and then waking at 4:30am with the answer. I know that between God and our subconscious working on the problem, ideas will come.

When you awake the next morning, before you look at any device, spend time thinking about your obstacle. Keep a prayer in your heart throughout the day and ask God to help you see or hear the solution. Write down any additional ideas or impressions below that may come to you. Then tweak it or find someone who can help you.

_____
_____
_____
_____
_____

Keep working and moving forward. If you find a closed door, trust that God has a better door for you to walk toward and keep your momentum going. You can also shift your focus to another mini goal until you the way opens. Pray and God will guide you.

END OF WEEK SUMMARY: WEEK __

And all things, whatsoever ye shall ask in prayer, believing, ye shall receive.

MATTHEW 21:22

God knows you and your situation perfectly. Remember the principle of grace as you review your week, and don't be hard on yourself.

What mini-goals did I accomplish this week?

_____
_____
_____
_____

What rewards did I enjoy?

_____
_____
_____
_____

What other things did I accomplish this week?

_____
_____
_____
_____

Are there any mini-goals that need to be modified or carried over to next week?

_____
_____
_____
_____

MY MIRACLES: Obstacles I have overcome this week and other ways I have seen God's hand.

_____
_____
_____
_____
_____

Obstacles I have *"given to God"* for further illumination:

_____
_____
_____
_____

NOTES: _____
_____
_____
_____
_____
_____
_____
_____
_____
_____
_____
_____
_____
_____

END OF MONTH SUMMARY

The desire accomplished is sweet to the soul.

PROVERBS 13:19

Fill in your data from this month's weekly goal sheets here.

What mini-goals did I accomplish this month?

_____
_____
_____
_____
_____
_____
_____
_____
_____
_____
_____

What rewards did I enjoy?

_____
_____
_____
_____
_____

What other things did I accomplish this month?

_____

MY MIRACLES: Obstacles I have overcome this month and other ways I have seen God's hand:

_____

How have I changed?

_____
_____
_____
_____
_____
_____
_____
_____
_____
_____

What mini-goals do I want to work on next month to keep moving forward?

_____
_____
_____
_____
_____
_____
_____
_____
_____

Will you please email me at **tamarakandersonauthor@gmail.com** to tell me about your accomplishments this month? I'd love to rejoice with you in your success!

NOTES:

END OF FIRST QUARTER SUMMARY

For I know the thoughts that I think toward you, saith the LORD, thoughts of peace, and not of evil, to give you an expected end.

JEREMIAH 29:11

Fill in your data from this quarter's monthly goal sheets here.　　　DATE: _____

What mini-goals did I accomplish this during the last three months?

What rewards did I enjoy?

What other things did I accomoplish?

MY MIRACLES: Obstacles I have overcome during the past 3 months and other ways I have seen God's hand:

How have I changed?

What mini-goals do I want to work on during the next quarter to keep moving forward?

SECOND QUARTER
Goal Worksheets

GOALS: WEEK ___

Trust in the Lord, and do good.

PSALM 37:3

My Inspired Resolution: DATE: _____

_____

MINI-GOALS – What I will accomplish this week + reward for each goal:

_____

_____

_____

_____

Now, **talk to God about it**. Tell Him about your weekly goals and ask for courage, faith, and patience to accomplish them.

Begin each morning with prayer. Tell God about your mini-goals and ask for the wisdom and determination to accomplish them. Schedule how you will work on one of your mini-goals that day and do it! Meditate and envision yourself accomplishing each goal and enjoying your reward.

Don't be discouraged if life throws curve balls at you during the day. Life happens. Give yourself grace and keep going. Learn more about how to overcome obstacles on the next page.

End every day with a prayer of thanks and a report of how you have done with your goals that day.

List any additional ideas or thoughts after your prayers below.

_____

_____

_____

Be flexible enough to incorporate additional ideas into your weekly goals. This is how you learn to trust God and be spontaneous enough to walk through doors that come up mid-week.

OBSTACLES: WEEK __

For this thing I besought the Lord thrice, that it might depart from me.

2 CORINTHIANS 12:8

During the week, take a few moments to evaluate this question:

What obstacles am I facing? _____

_____

_____

_____

_____

Talk to God at night about these obstacles and ask for His help. Turning it over to God doesn't mean you do nothing, but that you don't need to stress or worry. With God as your partner, you know you just need to do what you are able to do and leave the rest in His hands.

I have had some amazing experiences going to sleep with an obstacle or question and then waking at 4:30am with the answer. I know that between God and our subconscious working on the problem, ideas will come.

When you awake the next morning, before you look at any device, spend time thinking about your obstacle. Keep a prayer in your heart throughout the day and ask God to help you see or hear the solution. Write down any additional ideas or impressions below that may come to you. Then tweak it or find someone who can help you.

_____

_____

_____

_____

_____

Keep working and moving forward. If you find a closed door, trust that God has a better door for you to walk toward and keep your momentum going. You can also shift your focus to another mini goal until you the way opens. Pray and God will guide you.

END OF WEEK SUMMARY: WEEK __

But SEEK YE FIRST THE KINGDOM OF GOD, *and his righteousness; and all these things shall be added unto you.*

MATTHEW 6:33

God knows you and your situation perfectly. Remember the principle of grace as you review your week, and don't be hard on yourself.

What mini-goals did I accomplish this week?

_____
_____
_____
_____

What rewards did I enjoy?

_____
_____
_____
_____

What other things did I accomplish this week?

_____
_____
_____
_____

Are there any mini-goals that need to be modified or carried over to next week?

_____
_____
_____

MY MIRACLES: Obstacles I have overcome this week and other ways I have seen God's hand.

_____
_____
_____
_____
_____
_____

Obstacles I have *"given to God"* for further illumination:

_____
_____
_____
_____
_____

NOTES: _____
_____
_____
_____
_____
_____
_____
_____
_____
_____
_____
_____
_____
_____
_____

GOALS: WEEK __

I can do all things through Christ which strengtheneth me.

PHILIPPIANS 4:13

My Inspired Resolution: DATE: _____

_____

MINI-GOALS – What I will accomplish this week + reward for each goal:

_____

_____

_____

_____

Now, **talk to God about it**. Tell Him about your weekly goals and ask for courage, faith, and patience to accomplish them.

Begin each morning with prayer. Tell God about your mini-goals and ask for the wisdom and determination to accomplish them. Schedule how you will work on one of your mini-goals that day and do it! Meditate and envision yourself accomplishing each goal and enjoying your reward.

Don't be discouraged if life throws curve balls at you during the day. Life happens. Give yourself grace and keep going. Learn more about how to overcome obstacles on the next page.

End every day with a prayer of thanks and a report of how you have done with your goals that day.

List any additional ideas or thoughts after your prayers below.

_____

_____

_____

Be flexible enough to incorporate additional ideas into your weekly goals. This is how you learn to trust God and be spontaneous enough to walk through doors that come up mid-week.

OBSTACLES: WEEK __

We glory in tribulations also: knowing that tribulation worketh patience.

ROMANS 5:3

During the week, take a few moments to evaluate this question:

What obstacles am I facing? _____

_____

_____

_____

_____

Talk to God at night about these obstacles and ask for His help. Turning it over to God doesn't mean you do nothing, but that you don't need to stress or worry. With God as your partner, you know you just need to do what you are able to do and leave the rest in His hands.

I have had some amazing experiences going to sleep with an obstacle or question and then waking at 4:30am with the answer. I know that between God and our subconscious working on the problem, ideas will come.

When you awake the next morning, before you look at any device, spend time thinking about your obstacle. Keep a prayer in your heart throughout the day and ask God to help you see or hear the solution. Write down any additional ideas or impressions below that may come to you. Then tweak it or find someone who can help you.

_____

_____

_____

_____

_____

Keep working and moving forward. If you find a closed door, trust that God has a better door for you to walk toward and keep your momentum going. You can also shift your focus to another mini goal until you the way opens. Pray and God will guide you.

END OF WEEK SUMMARY: WEEK __

Know ye not that they which run in a race run all, but one receiveth the prize? So run, that ye may obtain.

1 CORINTHIANS 9:24

God knows you and your situation perfectly. Remember the principle of grace as you review your week, and don't be hard on yourself.

What mini-goals did I accomplish this week?

_____
_____
_____
_____

What rewards did I enjoy?

_____
_____
_____
_____

What other things did I accomplish this week?

_____
_____
_____
_____

Are there any mini-goals that need to be modified or carried over to next week?

_____
_____
_____

MY MIRACLES: Obstacles I have overcome this week and other ways I have seen God's hand.

Obstacles I have *"given to God"* for further illumination:

NOTES:

GOALS: WEEK __

All that the Lord hath said will we do.

EXODUS 24:7

My Inspired Resolution: DATE: _____

MINI-GOALS – What I will accomplish this week + reward for each goal:

Now, **talk to God about it**. Tell Him about your weekly goals and ask for courage, faith, and patience to accomplish them.

Begin each morning with prayer. Tell God about your mini-goals and ask for the wisdom and determination to accomplish them. Schedule how you will work on one of your mini-goals that day and do it! Meditate and envision yourself accomplishing each goal and enjoying your reward.

Don't be discouraged if life throws curve balls at you during the day. Life happens. Give yourself grace and keep going. Learn more about how to overcome obstacles on the next page.

End every day with a prayer of thanks and a report of how you have done with your goals that day.

List any additional ideas or thoughts after your prayers below.

Be flexible enough to incorporate additional ideas into your weekly goals. This is how you learn to trust God and be spontaneous enough to walk through doors that come up mid-week.

OBSTACLES: WEEK __

If ye have faith as a grain of mustard seed, ye shall say unto this mountain, Remove hence to yonder place; and it shall remove; and nothing shall be impossible unto you.

MATTHEW 17:20

During the week, take a few moments to evaluate this question:

What obstacles am I facing? _____

_____

_____

_____

_____

Talk to God at night about these obstacles and ask for His help. Turning it over to God doesn't mean you do nothing, but that you don't need to stress or worry. With God as your partner, you know you just need to do what you are able to do and leave the rest in His hands.

I have had some amazing experiences going to sleep with an obstacle or question and then waking at 4:30am with the answer. I know that between God and our subconscious working on the problem, ideas will come.

When you awake the next morning, before you look at any device, spend time thinking about your obstacle. Keep a prayer in your heart throughout the day and ask God to help you see or hear the solution. Write down any additional ideas or impressions below that may come to you. Then tweak it or find someone who can help you.

_____

_____

_____

_____

_____

Keep working and moving forward. If you find a closed door, trust that God has a better door for you to walk toward and keep your momentum going. You can also shift your focus to another mini goal until you the way opens. Pray and God will guide you.

END OF WEEK SUMMARY: WEEK __

Fear thou not; for I am with thee: be not dismayed; for I am thy God: I will strengthen thee; yea, I will help thee; yea, I will uphold thee with the right hand of my righteousness.

ISAIAH 41:10

God knows you and your situation perfectly. Remember the principle of grace as you review your week, and don't be hard on yourself.

What mini-goals did I accomplish this week?

_____
_____
_____
_____

What rewards did I enjoy?

_____
_____
_____
_____

What other things did I accomplish this week?

_____
_____
_____
_____

Are there any mini-goals that need to be modified or carried over to next week?

_____
_____
_____

MY MIRACLES: Obstacles I have overcome this week and other ways I have seen God's hand.

_____
_____
_____
_____
_____

Obstacles I have *"given to God"* for further illumination:

_____
_____
_____
_____

NOTES: _____
_____
_____
_____
_____
_____
_____
_____
_____
_____
_____
_____
_____

GOALS: WEEK ___

Trust in the Lord with all thine heart; and lean not unto thine own understanding. In all thy ways acknowledge Him, and He shall direct thy paths.

PROVERBS 3:5-6

My Inspired Resolution: DATE: _____

MINI-GOALS – What I will accomplish this week + reward for each goal:

Now, **talk to God about it**. Tell Him about your weekly goals and ask for courage, faith, and patience to accomplish them.

Begin each morning with prayer. Tell God about your mini-goals and ask for the wisdom and determination to accomplish them. Schedule how you will work on one of your mini-goals that day and do it! Meditate and envision yourself accomplishing each goal and enjoying your reward.

Don't be discouraged if life throws curve balls at you during the day. Life happens. Give yourself grace and keep going. Learn more about how to overcome obstacles on the next page.

End every day with a prayer of thanks and a report of how you have done with your goals that day.

List any additional ideas or thoughts after your prayers below.

Be flexible enough to incorporate additional ideas into your weekly goals. This is how you learn to trust God and be spontaneous enough to walk through doors that come up mid-week.

OBSTACLES: WEEK __

Prepare the way, take up the stumblingblock out of the way of my people.

ISAIAH 57:14

During the week, take a few moments to evaluate this question:

What obstacles am I facing? _____

_____

_____

_____

_____

Talk to God at night about these obstacles and ask for His help. Turning it over to God doesn't mean you do nothing, but that you don't need to stress or worry. With God as your partner, you know you just need to do what you are able to do and leave the rest in His hands.

I have had some amazing experiences going to sleep with an obstacle or question and then waking at 4:30am with the answer. I know that between God and our subconscious working on the problem, ideas will come.

When you awake the next morning, before you look at any device, spend time thinking about your obstacle. Keep a prayer in your heart throughout the day and ask God to help you see or hear the solution. Write down any additional ideas or impressions below that may come to you. Then tweak it or find someone who can help you.

_____

_____

_____

_____

_____

Keep working and moving forward. If you find a closed door, trust that God has a better door for you to walk toward and keep your momentum going. You can also shift your focus to another mini goal until you the way opens. Pray and God will guide you.

END OF WEEK SUMMARY: WEEK __

Commit thy works unto the Lord, and thy thoughts shall be established.

PROVERBS 16:3

God knows you and your situation perfectly. Remember the principle of grace as you review your week, and don't be hard on yourself.

What mini-goals did I accomplish this week?

_____
_____
_____
_____

What rewards did I enjoy?

_____
_____
_____
_____

What other things did I accomplish this week?

_____
_____
_____
_____

Are there any mini-goals that need to be modified or carried over to next week?

_____
_____
_____
_____

MY MIRACLES: Obstacles I have overcome this week and other ways I have seen God's hand.

_____
_____
_____
_____
_____

Obstacles I have *"given to God"* for further illumination:

_____
_____
_____
_____

NOTES: _____
_____
_____
_____
_____
_____
_____
_____
_____
_____
_____
_____
_____

GOALS: WEEK __

For God hath not given us the spirit of fear; but of power, and of love, and of a sound mind.

2 TIMOTHY 1:7

My Inspired Resolution: DATE: _____

_____

MINI-GOALS – What I will accomplish this week + reward for each goal:

_____

_____

_____

_____

Now, **talk to God about it**. Tell Him about your weekly goals and ask for courage, faith, and patience to accomplish them.

Begin each morning with prayer. Tell God about your mini-goals and ask for the wisdom and determination to accomplish them. Schedule how you will work on one of your mini-goals that day and do it! Meditate and envision yourself accomplishing each goal and enjoying your reward.

Don't be discouraged if life throws curve balls at you during the day. Life happens. Give yourself grace and keep going. Learn more about how to overcome obstacles on the next page.

End every day with a prayer of thanks and a report of how you have done with your goals that day.

List any additional ideas or thoughts after your prayers below.

_____

_____

_____

_____

Be flexible enough to incorporate additional ideas into your weekly goals. This is how you learn to trust God and be spontaneous enough to walk through doors that come up mid-week.

OBSTACLES: WEEK __

The LORD shall fight for you, and ye shall hold your peace.

EXODUS 14:14

During the week, take a few moments to evaluate this question:

What obstacles am I facing? _____

_____

_____

_____

_____

Talk to God at night about these obstacles and ask for His help. Turning it over to God doesn't mean you do nothing, but that you don't need to stress or worry. With God as your partner, you know you just need to do what you are able to do and leave the rest in His hands.

I have had some amazing experiences going to sleep with an obstacle or question and then waking at 4:30am with the answer. I know that between God and our subconscious working on the problem, ideas will come.

When you awake the next morning, before you look at any device, spend time thinking about your obstacle. Keep a prayer in your heart throughout the day and ask God to help you see or hear the solution. Write down any additional ideas or impressions below that may come to you. Then tweak it or find someone who can help you.

_____

_____

_____

_____

_____

Keep working and moving forward. If you find a closed door, trust that God has a better door for you to walk toward and keep your momentum going. You can also shift your focus to another mini goal until you the way opens. Pray and God will guide you.

END OF WEEK SUMMARY: WEEK __

A man's heart deviseth his way: but the Lord directeth his steps.

PROVERBS 16:9

God knows you and your situation perfectly. Remember the principle of grace as you review your week, and don't be hard on yourself.

What mini-goals did I accomplish this week?

_____
_____
_____
_____

What rewards did I enjoy?

_____
_____
_____
_____

What other things did I accomplish this week?

_____
_____
_____
_____

Are there any mini-goals that need to be modified or carried over to next week?

_____
_____
_____
_____

MY MIRACLES: Obstacles I have overcome this week and other ways I have seen God's hand.

_____
_____
_____
_____
_____

Obstacles I have *"given to God"* for further illumination:

_____
_____
_____
_____

NOTES: _____

_____
_____
_____
_____
_____
_____
_____
_____
_____
_____
_____

END OF MONTH SUMMARY

In all thy ways acknowledge him, and he shall direct thy paths.

PROVERBS 3:6

Fill in your data from this month's weekly goal sheets here.

What mini-goals did I accomplish this month?

_____
_____
_____
_____
_____
_____
_____
_____
_____
_____
_____

What rewards did I enjoy?

_____
_____
_____
_____
_____

What other things did I accomplish this month?

MY MIRACLES: Obstacles I have overcome this month and other ways I have seen God's hand:

How have I changed?

What mini-goals do I want to work on next month to keep moving forward?

Will you please email me at **tamarakandersonauthor@gmail.com** to tell me about your accomplishments this month? I'd love to rejoice with you in your success!

NOTES:

GOALS: WEEK ___

Shew me thy ways, O Lord; teach me thy paths.

PSALM 25:4

My Inspired Resolution: DATE: _____

MINI-GOALS – What I will accomplish this week + reward for each goal:

Now, **talk to God about it.** Tell Him about your weekly goals and ask for courage, faith, and patience to accomplish them.

Begin each morning with prayer. Tell God about your mini-goals and ask for the wisdom and determination to accomplish them. Schedule how you will work on one of your mini-goals that day and do it! Meditate and envision yourself accomplishing each goal and enjoying your reward.

Don't be discouraged if life throws curve balls at you during the day. Life happens. Give yourself grace and keep going. Learn more about how to overcome obstacles on the next page.

End every day with a prayer of thanks and a report of how you have done with your goals that day.

List any additional ideas or thoughts after your prayers below.

Be flexible enough to incorporate additional ideas into your weekly goals. This is how you learn to trust God and be spontaneous enough to walk through doors that come up mid-week.

OBSTACLES: WEEK __

In the world ye shall have tribulation: but be of good cheer; I have overcome the world.
JOHN 16:33

During the week, take a few moments to evaluate this question:

What obstacles am I facing? _____

_____
_____
_____
_____

Talk to God at night about these obstacles and ask for His help. Turning it over to God doesn't mean you do nothing, but that you don't need to stress or worry. With God as your partner, you know you just need to do what you are able to do and leave the rest in His hands.

I have had some amazing experiences going to sleep with an obstacle or question and then waking at 4:30am with the answer. I know that between God and our subconscious working on the problem, ideas will come.

When you awake the next morning, before you look at any device, spend time thinking about your obstacle. Keep a prayer in your heart throughout the day and ask God to help you see or hear the solution. Write down any additional ideas or impressions below that may come to you. Then tweak it or find someone who can help you.

_____
_____
_____
_____
_____
_____

Keep working and moving forward. If you find a closed door, trust that God has a better door for you to walk toward and keep your momentum going. You can also shift your focus to another mini goal until you the way opens. Pray and God will guide you.

END OF WEEK SUMMARY: WEEK __

Where there is no vision, the people perish.

PROVERBS 29:18

God knows you and your situation perfectly. Remember the principle of grace as you review your week, and don't be hard on yourself.

What mini-goals did I accomplish this week?

_____
_____
_____
_____

What rewards did I enjoy?

_____
_____
_____
_____

What other things did I accomplish this week?

_____
_____
_____
_____

Are there any mini-goals that need to be modified or carried over to next week?

_____
_____
_____
_____

MY MIRACLES: Obstacles I have overcome this week and other ways I have seen God's hand.

_____
_____
_____
_____
_____

Obstacles I have *"given to God"* for further illumination:

_____
_____
_____
_____

NOTES: _____
_____
_____
_____
_____
_____
_____
_____
_____
_____
_____
_____
_____

GOALS: WEEK ___

The Lord is my shepherd. I shall not want ... He leadeth me in the paths of righteousness ... I will fear no evil: for thou art with me.

PSALM 23: 1, 3, 4

My Inspired Resolution: DATE: _____

_____

MINI-GOALS – What I will accomplish this week + reward for each goal:

_____

_____

_____

Now, **talk to God about it**. Tell Him about your weekly goals and ask for courage, faith, and patience to accomplish them.

Begin each morning with prayer. Tell God about your mini-goals and ask for the wisdom and determination to accomplish them. Schedule how you will work on one of your mini-goals that day and do it! Meditate and envision yourself accomplishing each goal and enjoying your reward.

Don't be discouraged if life throws curve balls at you during the day. Life happens. Give yourself grace and keep going. Learn more about how to overcome obstacles on the next page.

End every day with a prayer of thanks and a report of how you have done with your goals that day.

List any additional ideas or thoughts after your prayers below.

_____

_____

_____

Be flexible enough to incorporate additional ideas into your weekly goals. This is how you learn to trust God and be spontaneous enough to walk through doors that come up mid-week.

OBSTACLES: WEEK __

Be not overcome of evil, but overcome evil with good.

ROMANS 12:21

During the week, take a few moments to evaluate this question:

What obstacles am I facing? _____

_____

_____

_____

_____

Talk to God at night about these obstacles and ask for His help. Turning it over to God doesn't mean you do nothing, but that you don't need to stress or worry. With God as your partner, you know you just need to do what you are able to do and leave the rest in His hands.

I have had some amazing experiences going to sleep with an obstacle or question and then waking at 4:30am with the answer. I know that between God and our subconscious working on the problem, ideas will come.

When you awake the next morning, before you look at any device, spend time thinking about your obstacle. Keep a prayer in your heart throughout the day and ask God to help you see or hear the solution. Write down any additional ideas or impressions below that may come to you. Then tweak it or find someone who can help you.

_____

_____

_____

_____

_____

Keep working and moving forward. If you find a closed door, trust that God has a better door for you to walk toward and keep your momentum going. You can also shift your focus to another mini goal until you the way opens. Pray and God will guide you.

END OF WEEK SUMMARY: WEEK __

I press toward the mark.

PHILIPPIANS 3:14

God knows you and your situation perfectly. Remember the principle of grace as you review your week, and don't be hard on yourself.

What mini-goals did I accomplish this week?

_____
_____
_____
_____

What rewards did I enjoy?

_____
_____
_____
_____

What other things did I accomplish this week?

_____
_____
_____
_____

Are there any mini-goals that need to be modified or carried over to next week?

_____
_____
_____
_____

MY MIRACLES: Obstacles I have overcome this week and other ways I have seen God's hand.

_____
_____
_____
_____
_____

Obstacles I have *"given to God"* for further illumination:

_____
_____
_____
_____

NOTES: _____
_____
_____
_____
_____
_____
_____
_____
_____
_____
_____
_____
_____
_____

GOALS: WEEK __

For this God is our God for ever and ever: He will be our guide even unto death.

PSALM 48:14

My Inspired Resolution: DATE: _____

MINI-GOALS – What I will accomplish this week + reward for each goal:

Now, **talk to God about it**. Tell Him about your weekly goals and ask for courage, faith, and patience to accomplish them.

Begin each morning with prayer. Tell God about your mini-goals and ask for the wisdom and determination to accomplish them. Schedule how you will work on one of your mini-goals that day and do it! Meditate and envision yourself accomplishing each goal and enjoying your reward.

Don't be discouraged if life throws curve balls at you during the day. Life happens. Give yourself grace and keep going. Learn more about how to overcome obstacles on the next page.

End every day with a prayer of thanks and a report of how you have done with your goals that day.

List any additional ideas or thoughts after your prayers below.

Be flexible enough to incorporate additional ideas into your weekly goals. This is how you learn to trust God and be spontaneous enough to walk through doors that come up mid-week.

OBSTACLES: WEEK __

Thanks be to God, which giveth us the victory through our Lord Jesus Christ.

1 CORINTHIANS 15:57

During the week, take a few moments to evaluate this question:

What obstacles am I facing? _____

_____
_____
_____
_____

Talk to God at night about these obstacles and ask for His help. Turning it over to God doesn't mean you do nothing, but that you don't need to stress or worry. With God as your partner, you know you just need to do what you are able to do and leave the rest in His hands.

I have had some amazing experiences going to sleep with an obstacle or question and then waking at 4:30am with the answer. I know that between God and our subconscious working on the problem, ideas will come.

When you awake the next morning, before you look at any device, spend time thinking about your obstacle. Keep a prayer in your heart throughout the day and ask God to help you see or hear the solution. Write down any additional ideas or impressions below that may come to you. Then tweak it or find someone who can help you.

_____
_____
_____
_____
_____

Keep working and moving forward. If you find a closed door, trust that God has a better door for you to walk toward and keep your momentum going. You can also shift your focus to another mini goal until you the way opens. Pray and God will guide you.

END OF WEEK SUMMARY: WEEK __

Commit thy way unto the LORD; trust also in him; and he shall bring it to pass.

PSALM 37:5

God knows you and your situation perfectly. Remember the principle of grace as you review your week, and don't be hard on yourself.

What mini-goals did I accomplish this week?

_____
_____
_____
_____

What rewards did I enjoy?

_____
_____
_____
_____

What other things did I accomplish this week?

_____
_____
_____
_____

Are there any mini-goals that need to be modified or carried over to next week?

_____
_____
_____
_____

MY MIRACLES: Obstacles I have overcome this week and other ways I have seen God's hand.

Obstacles I have *"given to God"* for further illumination:

NOTES:

GOALS: WEEK ___

For thou art my rock and my fortress;
therefore for thy name's sake lead me, and guide me.

PSALM 31:3

My Inspired Resolution: DATE: _____

_____

MINI-GOALS – What I will accomplish this week + reward for each goal:

_____

_____

_____

_____

Now, **talk to God about it**. Tell Him about your weekly goals and ask for courage, faith, and patience to accomplish them.

Begin each morning with prayer. Tell God about your mini-goals and ask for the wisdom and determination to accomplish them. Schedule how you will work on one of your mini-goals that day and do it! Meditate and envision yourself accomplishing each goal and enjoying your reward.

Don't be discouraged if life throws curve balls at you during the day. Life happens. Give yourself grace and keep going. Learn more about how to overcome obstacles on the next page.

End every day with a prayer of thanks and a report of how you have done with your goals that day.

List any additional ideas or thoughts after your prayers below.

_____

_____

_____

Be flexible enough to incorporate additional ideas into your weekly goals. This is how you learn to trust God and be spontaneous enough to walk through doors that come up mid-week.

OBSTACLES: WEEK __

In all these things we are more than conquerors through him that loved us.

ROMANS 8:37

During the week, take a few moments to evaluate this question:

What obstacles am I facing? _____

_____
_____
_____
_____

Talk to God at night about these obstacles and ask for His help. Turning it over to God doesn't mean you do nothing, but that you don't need to stress or worry. With God as your partner, you know you just need to do what you are able to do and leave the rest in His hands.

I have had some amazing experiences going to sleep with an obstacle or question and then waking at 4:30am with the answer. I know that between God and our subconscious working on the problem, ideas will come.

When you awake the next morning, before you look at any device, spend time thinking about your obstacle. Keep a prayer in your heart throughout the day and ask God to help you see or hear the solution. Write down any additional ideas or impressions below that may come to you. Then tweak it or find someone who can help you.

_____
_____
_____
_____
_____

Keep working and moving forward. If you find a closed door, trust that God has a better door for you to walk toward and keep your momentum going. You can also shift your focus to another mini goal until you the way opens. Pray and God will guide you.

END OF WEEK SUMMARY: WEEK __

Be ye strong therefore, and let not your hands be weak: for your work shall be rewarded.

2 CHRONICLES 15:7

God knows you and your situation perfectly. Remember the principle of grace as you review your week, and don't be hard on yourself.

What mini-goals did I accomplish this week?

_____
_____
_____
_____

What rewards did I enjoy?

_____
_____
_____
_____

What other things did I accomplish this week?

_____
_____
_____
_____

Are there any mini-goals that need to be modified or carried over to next week?

_____
_____
_____
_____

MY MIRACLES: Obstacles I have overcome this week and other ways I have seen God's hand.

_____
_____
_____
_____
_____
_____

Obstacles I have *"given to God"* for further illumination:

_____
_____
_____
_____
_____

NOTES: _____
_____
_____
_____
_____
_____
_____
_____
_____
_____
_____
_____
_____
_____
_____

GOALS: WEEK ___

Guide our feet into the way of peace.

LUKE 1:79

My Inspired Resolution: DATE: _____

MINI-GOALS – What I will accomplish this week + reward for each goal:

_____

_____

_____

_____

_____

Now, **talk to God about it**. Tell Him about your weekly goals and ask for courage, faith, and patience to accomplish them.

Begin each morning with prayer. Tell God about your mini-goals and ask for the wisdom and determination to accomplish them. Schedule how you will work on one of your mini-goals that day and do it! Meditate and envision yourself accomplishing each goal and enjoying your reward.

Don't be discouraged if life throws curve balls at you during the day. Life happens. Give yourself grace and keep going. Learn more about how to overcome obstacles on the next page.

End every day with a prayer of thanks and a report of how you have done with your goals that day.

List any additional ideas or thoughts after your prayers below.

_____

_____

_____

_____

Be flexible enough to incorporate additional ideas into your weekly goals. This is how you learn to trust God and be spontaneous enough to walk through doors that come up mid-week.

OBSTACLES: WEEK __

Let us run with patience the race that is set before us.

HEBREWS 12:1

During the week, take a few moments to evaluate this question:

What obstacles am I facing? _____

_____
_____
_____
_____

Talk to God at night about these obstacles and ask for His help. Turning it over to God doesn't mean you do nothing, but that you don't need to stress or worry. With God as your partner, you know you just need to do what you are able to do and leave the rest in His hands.

I have had some amazing experiences going to sleep with an obstacle or question and then waking at 4:30am with the answer. I know that between God and our subconscious working on the problem, ideas will come.

When you awake the next morning, before you look at any device, spend time thinking about your obstacle. Keep a prayer in your heart throughout the day and ask God to help you see or hear the solution. Write down any additional ideas or impressions below that may come to you. Then tweak it or find someone who can help you.

_____
_____
_____
_____
_____

Keep working and moving forward. If you find a closed door, trust that God has a better door for you to walk toward and keep your momentum going. You can also shift your focus to another mini goal until you the way opens. Pray and God will guide you.

END OF WEEK SUMMARY: WEEK ___

Delight thyself also in the LORD; and he shall give thee the desires of thine heart.

PSALM 37:4

God knows you and your situation perfectly. Remember the principle of grace as you review your week, and don't be hard on yourself.

What mini-goals did I accomplish this week?

___

What rewards did I enjoy?

___

What other things did I accomplish this week?

___

Are there any mini-goals that need to be modified or carried over to next week?

___

MY MIRACLES: Obstacles I have overcome this week and other ways I have seen God's hand.

_____
_____
_____
_____
_____

Obstacles I have *"given to God"* for further illumination:

_____
_____
_____
_____

NOTES: _____
_____
_____
_____
_____
_____
_____
_____
_____
_____
_____
_____
_____

END OF MONTH SUMMARY

Cast not away therefore your confidence, ... For ye have need of patience, that, after ye have done the will of God, ye might receive the promise.

HEBREWS 10:35-36

Fill in your data from this month's weekly goal sheets here.

What mini-goals did I accomplish this month?

_____
_____
_____
_____
_____
_____
_____
_____
_____
_____

What rewards did I enjoy?

_____
_____
_____
_____
_____

What other things did I accomplish this month?

_____
_____
_____
_____
_____
_____
_____
_____
_____
_____
_____

MY MIRACLES: Obstacles I have overcome this month and other ways I have seen God's hand:

_____
_____
_____
_____
_____
_____
_____
_____
_____
_____
_____

How have I changed?

_____

_____

_____

_____

_____

_____

_____

_____

_____

_____

What mini-goals do I want to work on next month to keep moving forward?

_____

_____

_____

_____

_____

_____

_____

_____

_____

Will you please email me at **tamarakandersonauthor@gmail.com** to tell me about your accomplishments this month? I'd love to rejoice with you in your success!

NOTES:

GOALS: WEEK __

*I will instruct thee and teach thee in the way which thou shalt go:
I will guide thee with mine eye.*

PSALM 32:8

My Inspired Resolution: DATE: _____

_____

MINI-GOALS – What I will accomplish this week + reward for each goal:

_____

_____

_____

Now, **talk to God about it**. Tell Him about your weekly goals and ask for courage, faith, and patience to accomplish them.

Begin each morning with prayer. Tell God about your mini-goals and ask for the wisdom and determination to accomplish them. Schedule how you will work on one of your mini-goals that day and do it! Meditate and envision yourself accomplishing each goal and enjoying your reward.

Don't be discouraged if life throws curve balls at you during the day. Life happens. Give yourself grace and keep going. Learn more about how to overcome obstacles on the next page.

End every day with a prayer of thanks and a report of how you have done with your goals that day.

List any additional ideas or thoughts after your prayers below.

_____

_____

_____

Be flexible enough to incorporate additional ideas into your weekly goals. This is how you learn to trust God and be spontaneous enough to walk through doors that come up mid-week.

OBSTACLES: WEEK __

Fight the good fight of faith.

1 TIMOTHY 6:12

During the week, take a few moments to evaluate this question:

What obstacles am I facing? _____

_____

_____

_____

_____

Talk to God at night about these obstacles and ask for His help. Turning it over to God doesn't mean you do nothing, but that you don't need to stress or worry. With God as your partner, you know you just need to do what you are able to do and leave the rest in His hands.

I have had some amazing experiences going to sleep with an obstacle or question and then waking at 4:30am with the answer. I know that between God and our subconscious working on the problem, ideas will come.

When you awake the next morning, before you look at any device, spend time thinking about your obstacle. Keep a prayer in your heart throughout the day and ask God to help you see or hear the solution. Write down any additional ideas or impressions below that may come to you. Then tweak it or find someone who can help you.

_____

_____

_____

_____

_____

Keep working and moving forward. If you find a closed door, trust that God has a better door for you to walk toward and keep your momentum going. You can also shift your focus to another mini goal until you the way opens. Pray and God will guide you.

END OF WEEK SUMMARY: WEEK __

But Jesus beheld them, and said unto them,
With men this is impossible; but with God all things are possible.

MATTHEW 19:26

God knows you and your situation perfectly. Remember the principle of grace as you review your week, and don't be hard on yourself.

What mini-goals did I accomplish this week?

_____
_____
_____
_____

What rewards did I enjoy?

_____
_____
_____
_____

What other things did I accomplish this week?

_____
_____
_____

Are there any mini-goals that need to be modified or carried over to next week?

_____
_____
_____

MY MIRACLES: Obstacles I have overcome this week and other ways I have seen God's hand.

___

Obstacles I have *"given to God"* for further illumination:

___

NOTES:

GOALS: WEEK __

And we know that all things work together for good to them that love God, to them who are the called according to his purpose.

ROMANS 8:28

My Inspired Resolution: DATE: _____

MINI-GOALS – What I will accomplish this week + reward for each goal:

Now, **talk to God about it**. Tell Him about your weekly goals and ask for courage, faith, and patience to accomplish them.

Begin each morning with prayer. Tell God about your mini-goals and ask for the wisdom and determination to accomplish them. Schedule how you will work on one of your mini-goals that day and do it! Meditate and envision yourself accomplishing each goal and enjoying your reward.

Don't be discouraged if life throws curve balls at you during the day. Life happens. Give yourself grace and keep going. Learn more about how to overcome obstacles on the next page.

End every day with a prayer of thanks and a report of how you have done with your goals that day.

List any additional ideas or thoughts after your prayers below.

Be flexible enough to incorporate additional ideas into your weekly goals. This is how you learn to trust God and be spontaneous enough to walk through doors that come up mid-week.

OBSTACLES: WEEK __

*Ye are of God, little children, and have overcome them:
because greater is he that is in you, than he that is in the world.*

1 JOHN 4:4

During the week, take a few moments to evaluate this question:

What obstacles am I facing? _____

_____

_____

_____

_____

Talk to God at night about these obstacles and ask for His help. Turning it over to God doesn't mean you do nothing, but that you don't need to stress or worry. With God as your partner, you know you just need to do what you are able to do and leave the rest in His hands.

I have had some amazing experiences going to sleep with an obstacle or question and then waking at 4:30am with the answer. I know that between God and our subconscious working on the problem, ideas will come.

When you awake the next morning, before you look at any device, spend time thinking about your obstacle. Keep a prayer in your heart throughout the day and ask God to help you see or hear the solution. Write down any additional ideas or impressions below that may come to you. Then tweak it or find someone who can help you.

_____

_____

_____

_____

_____

Keep working and moving forward. If you find a closed door, trust that God has a better door for you to walk toward and keep your momentum going. You can also shift your focus to another mini goal until you the way opens. Pray and God will guide you.

END OF WEEK SUMMARY: WEEK __

Be ye transformed by the renewing of your mind, that ye may prove what is that good, and acceptable, and perfect, will of God.

ROMANS 12:2

God knows you and your situation perfectly. Remember the principle of grace as you review your week, and don't be hard on yourself.

What mini-goals did I accomplish this week?

_____

_____

_____

_____

What rewards did I enjoy?

_____

_____

_____

_____

What other things did I accomplish this week?

_____

_____

_____

_____

Are there any mini-goals that need to be modified or carried over to next week?

_____

_____

_____

_____

MY MIRACLES: Obstacles I have overcome this week and other ways I have seen God's hand.

_____
_____
_____
_____
_____
_____

Obstacles I have *"given to God"* for further illumination:

_____
_____
_____
_____

NOTES: _____

_____
_____
_____
_____
_____
_____
_____
_____
_____
_____
_____
_____

GOALS: WEEK __

But they that wait upon the Lord shall renew their strength; they shall mount up with wings as eagles; they shall run, and not be weary; and they shall walk, and not faint.

ISAIAH 40:31

My Inspired Resolution: DATE: _____

MINI-GOALS – What I will accomplish this week + reward for each goal:

_____

_____

_____

_____

Now, **talk to God about it**. Tell Him about your weekly goals and ask for courage, faith, and patience to accomplish them.

Begin each morning with prayer. Tell God about your mini-goals and ask for the wisdom and determination to accomplish them. Schedule how you will work on one of your mini-goals that day and do it! Meditate and envision yourself accomplishing each goal and enjoying your reward.

Don't be discouraged if life throws curve balls at you during the day. Life happens. Give yourself grace and keep going. Learn more about how to overcome obstacles on the next page.

End every day with a prayer of thanks and a report of how you have done with your goals that day.

List any additional ideas or thoughts after your prayers below.

_____

_____

_____

_____

Be flexible enough to incorporate additional ideas into your weekly goals. This is how you learn to trust God and be spontaneous enough to walk through doors that come up mid-week.

OBSTACLES: WEEK __

O Lord, I beseech thee, send now prosperity.

PSALM 118:25

During the week, take a few moments to evaluate this question:

What obstacles am I facing? _____

_____
_____
_____
_____

Talk to God at night about these obstacles and ask for His help. Turning it over to God doesn't mean you do nothing, but that you don't need to stress or worry. With God as your partner, you know you just need to do what you are able to do and leave the rest in His hands.

I have had some amazing experiences going to sleep with an obstacle or question and then waking at 4:30am with the answer. I know that between God and our subconscious working on the problem, ideas will come.

When you awake the next morning, before you look at any device, spend time thinking about your obstacle. Keep a prayer in your heart throughout the day and ask God to help you see or hear the solution. Write down any additional ideas or impressions below that may come to you. Then tweak it or find someone who can help you.

_____
_____
_____
_____
_____
_____

Keep working and moving forward. If you find a closed door, trust that God has a better door for you to walk toward and keep your momentum going. You can also shift your focus to another mini goal until you the way opens. Pray and God will guide you.

END OF WEEK SUMMARY: WEEK __

Whatsoever things are true, … honest, … just, … pure, … lovely, …good report; if there be any virtue, and if there be any praise, think on these things.

PHILIPPIANS 4:8

God knows you and your situation perfectly. Remember the principle of grace as you review your week, and don't be hard on yourself.

What mini-goals did I accomplish this week?

_____
_____
_____
_____

What rewards did I enjoy?

_____
_____
_____
_____

What other things did I accomplish this week?

_____
_____
_____
_____

Are there any mini-goals that need to be modified or carried over to next week?

_____
_____
_____

MY MIRACLES: Obstacles I have overcome this week and other ways I have seen God's hand.

_____
_____
_____
_____
_____

Obstacles I have *"given to God"* for further illumination:

_____
_____
_____
_____

NOTES: _____
_____
_____
_____
_____
_____
_____
_____
_____
_____
_____
_____
_____

GOALS: WEEK ___

Great is thy faithfulness. The Lord is my portion, saith my soul; therefore I will hope in him.
LAMENTATIONS 3:23-24

My Inspired Resolution: DATE: _____

_____

MINI-GOALS – What I will accomplish this week + reward for each goal:

_____

_____

_____

_____

Now, **talk to God about it**. Tell Him about your weekly goals and ask for courage, faith, and patience to accomplish them.

Begin each morning with prayer. Tell God about your mini-goals and ask for the wisdom and determination to accomplish them. Schedule how you will work on one of your mini-goals that day and do it! Meditate and envision yourself accomplishing each goal and enjoying your reward.

Don't be discouraged if life throws curve balls at you during the day. Life happens. Give yourself grace and keep going. Learn more about how to overcome obstacles on the next page.

End every day with a prayer of thanks and a report of how you have done with your goals that day.

List any additional ideas or thoughts after your prayers below.

_____

_____

_____

Be flexible enough to incorporate additional ideas into your weekly goals. This is how you learn to trust God and be spontaneous enough to walk through doors that come up mid-week.

OBSTACLES: WEEK __

Thou shalt preserve me from trouble; thou shalt compass me about with songs of deliverance.

PSALM 32:7

During the week, take a few moments to evaluate this question:

What obstacles am I facing? _____

_____

_____

_____

_____

Talk to God at night about these obstacles and ask for His help. Turning it over to God doesn't mean you do nothing, but that you don't need to stress or worry. With God as your partner, you know you just need to do what you are able to do and leave the rest in His hands.

I have had some amazing experiences going to sleep with an obstacle or question and then waking at 4:30am with the answer. I know that between God and our subconscious working on the problem, ideas will come.

When you awake the next morning, before you look at any device, spend time thinking about your obstacle. Keep a prayer in your heart throughout the day and ask God to help you see or hear the solution. Write down any additional ideas or impressions below that may come to you. Then tweak it or find someone who can help you.

_____

_____

_____

_____

_____

Keep working and moving forward. If you find a closed door, trust that God has a better door for you to walk toward and keep your momentum going. You can also shift your focus to another mini goal until you the way opens. Pray and God will guide you.

END OF WEEK SUMMARY: WEEK __

Jesus saith unto them, My meat is to do the will of him that sent me, and to finish his work.

JOHN 4:34

God knows you and your situation perfectly. Remember the principle of grace as you review your week, and don't be hard on yourself.

What mini-goals did I accomplish this week?

_____
_____
_____
_____

What rewards did I enjoy?

_____
_____
_____
_____

What other things did I accomplish this week?

_____
_____
_____
_____

Are there any mini-goals that need to be modified or carried over to next week?

_____
_____
_____
_____

MY MIRACLES: Obstacles I have overcome this week and other ways I have seen God's hand.

_____
_____
_____
_____
_____

Obstacles I have *"given to God"* for further illumination:

_____
_____
_____
_____
_____

NOTES: _____
_____
_____
_____
_____
_____
_____
_____
_____
_____
_____
_____
_____
_____

GOALS: WEEK ___

It is good that a man should both hope and quietly wait for the salvation of the Lord.

LAMENTATIONS 3:26

My Inspired Resolution: DATE: _____

MINI-GOALS – What I will accomplish this week + reward for each goal:

Now, **talk to God about it.** Tell Him about your weekly goals and ask for courage, faith, and patience to accomplish them.

Begin each morning with prayer. Tell God about your mini-goals and ask for the wisdom and determination to accomplish them. Schedule how you will work on one of your mini-goals that day and do it! Meditate and envision yourself accomplishing each goal and enjoying your reward.

Don't be discouraged if life throws curve balls at you during the day. Life happens. Give yourself grace and keep going. Learn more about how to overcome obstacles on the next page.

End every day with a prayer of thanks and a report of how you have done with your goals that day.

List any additional ideas or thoughts after your prayers below.

Be flexible enough to incorporate additional ideas into your weekly goals. This is how you learn to trust God and be spontaneous enough to walk through doors that come up mid-week.

OBSTACLES: WEEK __

And ye shall seek me, and find me, when ye shall search for me with all your heart.

JEREMIAH 29:13

During the week, take a few moments to evaluate this question:

What obstacles am I facing? _____

_____

_____

_____

_____

Talk to God at night about these obstacles and ask for His help. Turning it over to God doesn't mean you do nothing, but that you don't need to stress or worry. With God as your partner, you know you just need to do what you are able to do and leave the rest in His hands.

I have had some amazing experiences going to sleep with an obstacle or question and then waking at 4:30am with the answer. I know that between God and our subconscious working on the problem, ideas will come.

When you awake the next morning, before you look at any device, spend time thinking about your obstacle. Keep a prayer in your heart throughout the day and ask God to help you see or hear the solution. Write down any additional ideas or impressions below that may come to you. Then tweak it or find someone who can help you.

_____

_____

_____

_____

_____

Keep working and moving forward. If you find a closed door, trust that God has a better door for you to walk toward and keep your momentum going. You can also shift your focus to another mini goal until you the way opens. Pray and God will guide you.

END OF WEEK SUMMARY: WEEK __

And all things, whatsoever ye shall ask in prayer, believing, ye shall receive.

MATTHEW 21:22

God knows you and your situation perfectly. Remember the principle of grace as you review your week, and don't be hard on yourself.

What mini-goals did I accomplish this week?

_____
_____
_____
_____

What rewards did I enjoy?

_____
_____
_____
_____

What other things did I accomplish this week?

_____
_____
_____
_____

Are there any mini-goals that need to be modified or carried over to next week?

_____
_____
_____
_____

MY MIRACLES: Obstacles I have overcome this week and other ways I have seen God's hand.

_____
_____
_____
_____
_____
_____

Obstacles I have *"given to God"* for further illumination:

_____
_____
_____
_____
_____

NOTES: _____
_____
_____
_____
_____
_____
_____
_____
_____
_____
_____
_____
_____
_____

END OF MONTH SUMMARY

The desire accomplished is sweet to the soul.

PROVERBS 13:19

Fill in your data from this month's weekly goal sheets here.

What mini-goals did I accomplish this month?

_____
_____
_____
_____
_____
_____
_____
_____
_____
_____
_____
_____

What rewards did I enjoy?

_____
_____
_____
_____
_____

What other things did I accomplish this month?

MY MIRACLES: Obstacles I have overcome this month and other ways I have seen God's hand:

How have I changed?

What mini-goals do I want to work on next month to keep moving forward?

Will you please email me at **tamarakandersonauthor@gmail.com** to tell me about your accomplishments this month? I'd love to rejoice with you in your success!

NOTES:

END OF SECOND QUARTER SUMMARY

For I know the thoughts that I think toward you, saith the LORD, thoughts of peace, and not of evil, to give you an expected end.

JEREMIAH 29:11

Fill in your data from this quarter's monthly goal sheets here. DATE:

What mini-goals did I accomplish this during the last three months?

What rewards did I enjoy?

What other things did I accomoplish?

MY MIRACLES: Obstacles I have overcome during the past 3 months and other ways I have seen God's hand:

How have I changed?

What mini-goals do I want to work on during the next quarter to keep moving forward?

THIRD QUARTER
Goal Worksheets

GOALS: WEEK ___

Trust in the Lord, and do good.

PSALM 37:3

My Inspired Resolution: DATE: _____

_____

MINI-GOALS – What I will accomplish this week + reward for each goal:

_____

_____

_____

_____

Now, **talk to God about it**. Tell Him about your weekly goals and ask for courage, faith, and patience to accomplish them.

Begin each morning with prayer. Tell God about your mini-goals and ask for the wisdom and determination to accomplish them. Schedule how you will work on one of your mini-goals that day and do it! Meditate and envision yourself accomplishing each goal and enjoying your reward.

Don't be discouraged if life throws curve balls at you during the day. Life happens. Give yourself grace and keep going. Learn more about how to overcome obstacles on the next page.

End every day with a prayer of thanks and a report of how you have done with your goals that day.

List any additional ideas or thoughts after your prayers below.

_____

_____

_____

Be flexible enough to incorporate additional ideas into your weekly goals. This is how you learn to trust God and be spontaneous enough to walk through doors that come up mid-week.

OBSTACLES: WEEK __

For this thing I besought the Lord thrice, that it might depart from me.

2 CORINTHIANS 12:8

During the week, take a few moments to evaluate this question:

What obstacles am I facing? _____

_____

_____

_____

_____

Talk to God at night about these obstacles and ask for His help. Turning it over to God doesn't mean you do nothing, but that you don't need to stress or worry. With God as your partner, you know you just need to do what you are able to do and leave the rest in His hands.

I have had some amazing experiences going to sleep with an obstacle or question and then waking at 4:30am with the answer. I know that between God and our subconscious working on the problem, ideas will come.

When you awake the next morning, before you look at any device, spend time thinking about your obstacle. Keep a prayer in your heart throughout the day and ask God to help you see or hear the solution. Write down any additional ideas or impressions below that may come to you. Then tweak it or find someone who can help you.

_____

_____

_____

_____

_____

Keep working and moving forward. If you find a closed door, trust that God has a better door for you to walk toward and keep your momentum going. You can also shift your focus to another mini goal until you the way opens. Pray and God will guide you.

END OF WEEK SUMMARY: WEEK __

But SEEK YE FIRST THE KINGDOM OF GOD, *and his righteousness; and all these things shall be added unto you.*

MATTHEW 6:33

God knows you and your situation perfectly. Remember the principle of grace as you review your week, and don't be hard on yourself.

What mini-goals did I accomplish this week?

_____
_____
_____
_____

What rewards did I enjoy?

_____
_____
_____
_____

What other things did I accomplish this week?

_____
_____
_____
_____

Are there any mini-goals that need to be modified or carried over to next week?

_____
_____
_____

MY MIRACLES: Obstacles I have overcome this week and other ways I have seen God's hand.

_____
_____
_____
_____
_____

Obstacles I have *"given to God"* for further illumination:

_____
_____
_____
_____

NOTES: _____
_____
_____
_____
_____
_____
_____
_____
_____
_____
_____
_____

GOALS: WEEK __

I can do all things through Christ which strengtheneth me.

PHILIPPIANS 4:13

My Inspired Resolution: DATE: _____

MINI-GOALS – What I will accomplish this week + reward for each goal:

Now, **talk to God about it**. Tell Him about your weekly goals and ask for courage, faith, and patience to accomplish them.

Begin each morning with prayer. Tell God about your mini-goals and ask for the wisdom and determination to accomplish them. Schedule how you will work on one of your mini-goals that day and do it! Meditate and envision yourself accomplishing each goal and enjoying your reward.

Don't be discouraged if life throws curve balls at you during the day. Life happens. Give yourself grace and keep going. Learn more about how to overcome obstacles on the next page.

End every day with a prayer of thanks and a report of how you have done with your goals that day.

List any additional ideas or thoughts after your prayers below.

Be flexible enough to incorporate additional ideas into your weekly goals. This is how you learn to trust God and be spontaneous enough to walk through doors that come up mid-week.

OBSTACLES: WEEK __

We glory in tribulations also: knowing that tribulation worketh patience.

ROMANS 5:3

During the week, take a few moments to evaluate this question:

What obstacles am I facing? _____

_____
_____
_____
_____

Talk to God at night about these obstacles and ask for His help. Turning it over to God doesn't mean you do nothing, but that you don't need to stress or worry. With God as your partner, you know you just need to do what you are able to do and leave the rest in His hands.

I have had some amazing experiences going to sleep with an obstacle or question and then waking at 4:30am with the answer. I know that between God and our subconscious working on the problem, ideas will come.

When you awake the next morning, before you look at any device, spend time thinking about your obstacle. Keep a prayer in your heart throughout the day and ask God to help you see or hear the solution. Write down any additional ideas or impressions below that may come to you. Then tweak it or find someone who can help you.

_____
_____
_____
_____
_____

Keep working and moving forward. If you find a closed door, trust that God has a better door for you to walk toward and keep your momentum going. You can also shift your focus to another mini goal until you the way opens. Pray and God will guide you.

END OF WEEK SUMMARY: WEEK __

Know ye not that they which run in a race run all, but one receiveth the prize? So run, that ye may obtain.

1 CORINTHIANS 9:24

God knows you and your situation perfectly. Remember the principle of grace as you review your week, and don't be hard on yourself.

What mini-goals did I accomplish this week?

_____
_____
_____
_____

What rewards did I enjoy?

_____
_____
_____
_____

What other things did I accomplish this week?

_____
_____
_____
_____

Are there any mini-goals that need to be modified or carried over to next week?

_____
_____

MY MIRACLES: Obstacles I have overcome this week and other ways I have seen God's hand.

_____
_____
_____
_____
_____

Obstacles I have *"given to God"* for further illumination:

_____
_____
_____
_____

NOTES: _____

_____
_____
_____
_____
_____
_____
_____
_____
_____
_____
_____
_____

GOALS: WEEK ___

All that the Lord hath said will we do.

EXODUS 24:7

My Inspired Resolution: DATE: _____

MINI-GOALS – What I will accomplish this week + reward for each goal:

Now, **talk to God about it**. Tell Him about your weekly goals and ask for courage, faith, and patience to accomplish them.

Begin each morning with prayer. Tell God about your mini-goals and ask for the wisdom and determination to accomplish them. Schedule how you will work on one of your mini-goals that day and do it! Meditate and envision yourself accomplishing each goal and enjoying your reward.

Don't be discouraged if life throws curve balls at you during the day. Life happens. Give yourself grace and keep going. Learn more about how to overcome obstacles on the next page.

End every day with a prayer of thanks and a report of how you have done with your goals that day.

List any additional ideas or thoughts after your prayers below.

Be flexible enough to incorporate additional ideas into your weekly goals. This is how you learn to trust God and be spontaneous enough to walk through doors that come up mid-week.

OBSTACLES: WEEK __

If ye have faith as a grain of mustard seed, ye shall say unto this mountain, Remove hence to yonder place; and it shall remove; and nothing shall be impossible unto you.

MATTHEW 17:20

During the week, take a few moments to evaluate this question:

What obstacles am I facing? _____

_____

_____

_____

_____

Talk to God at night about these obstacles and ask for His help. Turning it over to God doesn't mean you do nothing, but that you don't need to stress or worry. With God as your partner, you know you just need to do what you are able to do and leave the rest in His hands.

I have had some amazing experiences going to sleep with an obstacle or question and then waking at 4:30am with the answer. I know that between God and our subconscious working on the problem, ideas will come.

When you awake the next morning, before you look at any device, spend time thinking about your obstacle. Keep a prayer in your heart throughout the day and ask God to help you see or hear the solution. Write down any additional ideas or impressions below that may come to you. Then tweak it or find someone who can help you.

_____

_____

_____

_____

_____

Keep working and moving forward. If you find a closed door, trust that God has a better door for you to walk toward and keep your momentum going. You can also shift your focus to another mini goal until you the way opens. Pray and God will guide you.

END OF WEEK SUMMARY: WEEK __

Fear thou not; for I am with thee: be not dismayed; for I am thy God: I will strengthen thee; yea, I will help thee; yea, I will uphold thee with the right hand of my righteousness.

ISAIAH 41:10

God knows you and your situation perfectly. Remember the principle of grace as you review your week, and don't be hard on yourself.

What mini-goals did I accomplish this week?

_____
_____
_____
_____

What rewards did I enjoy?

_____
_____
_____
_____

What other things did I accomplish this week?

_____
_____
_____
_____

Are there any mini-goals that need to be modified or carried over to next week?

_____
_____
_____
_____

MY MIRACLES: Obstacles I have overcome this week and other ways I have seen God's hand.

Obstacles I have *"given to God"* for further illumination:

NOTES:

GOALS: WEEK ___

Trust in the Lord with all thine heart; and lean not unto thine own understanding. In all thy ways acknowledge Him, and He shall direct thy paths.

PROVERBS 3:5-6

My Inspired Resolution: DATE: _____

_____

MINI-GOALS – What I will accomplish this week + reward for each goal:

_____
_____
_____
_____

Now, **talk to God about it**. Tell Him about your weekly goals and ask for courage, faith, and patience to accomplish them.

Begin each morning with prayer. Tell God about your mini-goals and ask for the wisdom and determination to accomplish them. Schedule how you will work on one of your mini-goals that day and do it! Meditate and envision yourself accomplishing each goal and enjoying your reward.

Don't be discouraged if life throws curve balls at you during the day. Life happens. Give yourself grace and keep going. Learn more about how to overcome obstacles on the next page.

End every day with a prayer of thanks and a report of how you have done with your goals that day.

List any additional ideas or thoughts after your prayers below.

_____
_____
_____
_____

Be flexible enough to incorporate additional ideas into your weekly goals. This is how you learn to trust God and be spontaneous enough to walk through doors that come up mid-week.

OBSTACLES: WEEK __

Prepare the way, take up the stumblingblock out of the way of my people.
ISAIAH 57:14

During the week, take a few moments to evaluate this question:

What obstacles am I facing? _____

_____
_____
_____
_____

Talk to God at night about these obstacles and ask for His help. Turning it over to God doesn't mean you do nothing, but that you don't need to stress or worry. With God as your partner, you know you just need to do what you are able to do and leave the rest in His hands.

I have had some amazing experiences going to sleep with an obstacle or question and then waking at 4:30am with the answer. I know that between God and our subconscious working on the problem, ideas will come.

When you awake the next morning, before you look at any device, spend time thinking about your obstacle. Keep a prayer in your heart throughout the day and ask God to help you see or hear the solution. Write down any additional ideas or impressions below that may come to you. Then tweak it or find someone who can help you.

_____
_____
_____
_____

Keep working and moving forward. If you find a closed door, trust that God has a better door for you to walk toward and keep your momentum going. You can also shift your focus to another mini goal until you the way opens. Pray and God will guide you.

END OF WEEK SUMMARY: WEEK __

Commit thy works unto the Lord, and thy thoughts shall be established.

PROVERBS 16:3

God knows you and your situation perfectly. Remember the principle of grace as you review your week, and don't be hard on yourself.

What mini-goals did I accomplish this week?

_____
_____
_____
_____

What rewards did I enjoy?

_____
_____
_____
_____

What other things did I accomplish this week?

_____
_____
_____
_____

Are there any mini-goals that need to be modified or carried over to next week?

_____
_____
_____
_____

MY MIRACLES: Obstacles I have overcome this week and other ways I have seen God's hand.

_____
_____
_____
_____
_____

Obstacles I have *"given to God"* for further illumination:

_____
_____
_____
_____

NOTES: _____

_____
_____
_____
_____
_____
_____
_____
_____
_____
_____
_____

GOALS: WEEK ___

For God hath not given us the spirit of fear; but of power, and of love, and of a sound mind."
2 TIMOTHY 1:7

My Inspired Resolution: DATE: _____

_____

MINI-GOALS – What I will accomplish this week + reward for each goal:

_____
_____
_____
_____

Now, **talk to God about it**. Tell Him about your weekly goals and ask for courage, faith, and patience to accomplish them.

Begin each morning with prayer. Tell God about your mini-goals and ask for the wisdom and determination to accomplish them. Schedule how you will work on one of your mini-goals that day and do it! Meditate and envision yourself accomplishing each goal and enjoying your reward.

Don't be discouraged if life throws curve balls at you during the day. Life happens. Give yourself grace and keep going. Learn more about how to overcome obstacles on the next page.

End every day with a prayer of thanks and a report of how you have done with your goals that day.

List any additional ideas or thoughts after your prayers below.

_____
_____
_____

Be flexible enough to incorporate additional ideas into your weekly goals. This is how you learn to trust God and be spontaneous enough to walk through doors that come up mid-week.

OBSTACLES: WEEK __

The LORD shall fight for you, and ye shall hold your peace.

EXODUS 14:14

During the week, take a few moments to evaluate this question:

What obstacles am I facing? _____

_____
_____
_____
_____

Talk to God at night about these obstacles and ask for His help. Turning it over to God doesn't mean you do nothing, but that you don't need to stress or worry. With God as your partner, you know you just need to do what you are able to do and leave the rest in His hands.

I have had some amazing experiences going to sleep with an obstacle or question and then waking at 4:30am with the answer. I know that between God and our subconscious working on the problem, ideas will come.

When you awake the next morning, before you look at any device, spend time thinking about your obstacle. Keep a prayer in your heart throughout the day and ask God to help you see or hear the solution. Write down any additional ideas or impressions below that may come to you. Then tweak it or find someone who can help you.

_____
_____
_____
_____
_____

Keep working and moving forward. If you find a closed door, trust that God has a better door for you to walk toward and keep your momentum going. You can also shift your focus to another mini goal until you the way opens. Pray and God will guide you.

END OF WEEK SUMMARY: WEEK ___

A man's heart deviseth his way: but the Lord directeth his steps.

PROVERBS 16:9

God knows you and your situation perfectly. Remember the principle of grace as you review your week, and don't be hard on yourself.

What mini-goals did I accomplish this week?

_____
_____
_____
_____

What rewards did I enjoy?

_____
_____
_____
_____

What other things did I accomplish this week?

_____
_____
_____
_____

Are there any mini-goals that need to be modified or carried over to next week?

_____
_____
_____
_____

MY MIRACLES: Obstacles I have overcome this week and other ways I have seen God's hand.

_____
_____
_____
_____
_____

Obstacles I have *"given to God"* for further illumination:

_____
_____
_____
_____

NOTES: _____
_____
_____
_____
_____
_____
_____
_____
_____
_____
_____
_____
_____

END OF MONTH SUMMARY

In all thy ways acknowledge him, and he shall direct thy paths.

PROVERBS 3:6

Fill in your data from this month's weekly goal sheets here.

What mini-goals did I accomplish this month?

_____
_____
_____
_____
_____
_____
_____
_____
_____
_____
_____

What rewards did I enjoy?

_____
_____
_____
_____
_____

What other things did I accomplish this month?

_____
_____
_____
_____
_____
_____
_____
_____
_____
_____
_____

MY MIRACLES: Obstacles I have overcome this month and other ways I have seen God's hand:

_____
_____
_____
_____
_____
_____
_____
_____
_____
_____
_____

How have I changed?

What mini-goals do I want to work on next month to keep moving forward?

Will you please email me at **tamarakandersonauthor@gmail.com** to tell me about your accomplishments this month? I'd love to rejoice with you in your success!

NOTES:

GOALS: WEEK ___

Shew me thy ways, O Lord; teach me thy paths.

PSALM 25:4

My Inspired Resolution: DATE: _____

MINI-GOALS – What I will accomplish this week + reward for each goal:

Now, **talk to God about it**. Tell Him about your weekly goals and ask for courage, faith, and patience to accomplish them.

Begin each morning with prayer. Tell God about your mini-goals and ask for the wisdom and determination to accomplish them. Schedule how you will work on one of your mini-goals that day and do it! Meditate and envision yourself accomplishing each goal and enjoying your reward.

Don't be discouraged if life throws curve balls at you during the day. Life happens. Give yourself grace and keep going. Learn more about how to overcome obstacles on the next page.

End every day with a prayer of thanks and a report of how you have done with your goals that day.

List any additional ideas or thoughts after your prayers below.

Be flexible enough to incorporate additional ideas into your weekly goals. This is how you learn to trust God and be spontaneous enough to walk through doors that come up mid-week.

OBSTACLES: WEEK __

In the world ye shall have tribulation: but be of good cheer; I have overcome the world.

JOHN 16:33

During the week, take a few moments to evaluate this question:

What obstacles am I facing? _____

_____

_____

_____

_____

Talk to God at night about these obstacles and ask for His help. Turning it over to God doesn't mean you do nothing, but that you don't need to stress or worry. With God as your partner, you know you just need to do what you are able to do and leave the rest in His hands.

I have had some amazing experiences going to sleep with an obstacle or question and then waking at 4:30am with the answer. I know that between God and our subconscious working on the problem, ideas will come.

When you awake the next morning, before you look at any device, spend time thinking about your obstacle. Keep a prayer in your heart throughout the day and ask God to help you see or hear the solution. Write down any additional ideas or impressions below that may come to you. Then tweak it or find someone who can help you.

_____

_____

_____

_____

_____

Keep working and moving forward. If you find a closed door, trust that God has a better door for you to walk toward and keep your momentum going. You can also shift your focus to another mini goal until you the way opens. Pray and God will guide you.

END OF WEEK SUMMARY: WEEK __

Where there is no vision, the people perish.
PROVERBS 29:18

God knows you and your situation perfectly. Remember the principle of grace as you review your week, and don't be hard on yourself.

What mini-goals did I accomplish this week?

_____
_____
_____
_____

What rewards did I enjoy?

_____
_____
_____
_____

What other things did I accomplish this week?

_____
_____
_____
_____

Are there any mini-goals that need to be modified or carried over to next week?

_____
_____
_____
_____

MY MIRACLES: Obstacles I have overcome this week and other ways I have seen God's hand.

_____
_____
_____
_____
_____

Obstacles I have *"given to God"* for further illumination:

_____
_____
_____
_____

NOTES: _____

_____
_____
_____
_____
_____
_____
_____
_____
_____
_____
_____

GOALS: WEEK ___

The Lord is my shepherd. I shall not want . . . He leadeth me in the paths of righteousness . . . I will fear no evil: for thou art with me.

PSALM 23: 1, 3, 4

My Inspired Resolution: DATE: _____

_____

MINI-GOALS – What I will accomplish this week + reward for each goal:

_____
_____
_____

Now, **talk to God about it**. Tell Him about your weekly goals and ask for courage, faith, and patience to accomplish them.

Begin each morning with prayer. Tell God about your mini-goals and ask for the wisdom and determination to accomplish them. Schedule how you will work on one of your mini-goals that day and do it! Meditate and envision yourself accomplishing each goal and enjoying your reward.

Don't be discouraged if life throws curve balls at you during the day. Life happens. Give yourself grace and keep going. Learn more about how to overcome obstacles on the next page.

End every day with a prayer of thanks and a report of how you have done with your goals that day.

List any additional ideas or thoughts after your prayers below.

_____
_____
_____

Be flexible enough to incorporate additional ideas into your weekly goals. This is how you learn to trust God and be spontaneous enough to walk through doors that come up mid-week.

OBSTACLES: WEEK __

Be not overcome of evil, but overcome evil with good.

ROMANS 12:21

During the week, take a few moments to evaluate this question:

What obstacles am I facing? _____

_____

_____

_____

_____

Talk to God at night about these obstacles and ask for His help. Turning it over to God doesn't mean you do nothing, but that you don't need to stress or worry. With God as your partner, you know you just need to do what you are able to do and leave the rest in His hands.

I have had some amazing experiences going to sleep with an obstacle or question and then waking at 4:30am with the answer. I know that between God and our subconscious working on the problem, ideas will come.

When you awake the next morning, before you look at any device, spend time thinking about your obstacle. Keep a prayer in your heart throughout the day and ask God to help you see or hear the solution. Write down any additional ideas or impressions below that may come to you. Then tweak it or find someone who can help you.

_____

_____

_____

_____

_____

Keep working and moving forward. If you find a closed door, trust that God has a better door for you to walk toward and keep your momentum going. You can also shift your focus to another mini goal until you the way opens. Pray and God will guide you.

END OF WEEK SUMMARY: WEEK __

I press toward the mark.

PHILIPPIANS 3:14

God knows you and your situation perfectly. Remember the principle of grace as you review your week, and don't be hard on yourself.

What mini-goals did I accomplish this week?

_____
_____
_____
_____

What rewards did I enjoy?

_____
_____
_____
_____

What other things did I accomplish this week?

_____
_____
_____
_____

Are there any mini-goals that need to be modified or carried over to next week?

_____
_____
_____
_____

MY MIRACLES: Obstacles I have overcome this week and other ways I have seen God's hand.

_____
_____
_____
_____
_____

Obstacles I have *"given to God"* for further illumination:

_____
_____
_____
_____
_____

NOTES: _____
_____
_____
_____
_____
_____
_____
_____
_____
_____
_____
_____
_____
_____
_____

GOALS: WEEK ___

For this God is our God for ever and ever: He will be our guide even unto death.

PSALM 48:14

My Inspired Resolution: DATE: _____

_____

MINI-GOALS – What I will accomplish this week + reward for each goal:

_____
_____
_____
_____

Now, **talk to God about it**. Tell Him about your weekly goals and ask for courage, faith, and patience to accomplish them.

Begin each morning with prayer. Tell God about your mini-goals and ask for the wisdom and determination to accomplish them. Schedule how you will work on one of your mini-goals that day and do it! Meditate and envision yourself accomplishing each goal and enjoying your reward.

Don't be discouraged if life throws curve balls at you during the day. Life happens. Give yourself grace and keep going. Learn more about how to overcome obstacles on the next page.

End every day with a prayer of thanks and a report of how you have done with your goals that day.

List any additional ideas or thoughts after your prayers below.

_____
_____
_____

Be flexible enough to incorporate additional ideas into your weekly goals. This is how you learn to trust God and be spontaneous enough to walk through doors that come up mid-week.

OBSTACLES: WEEK __

Thanks be to God, which giveth us the victory through our Lord Jesus Christ.

1 CORINTHIANS 15:57

During the week, take a few moments to evaluate this question:

What obstacles am I facing? _____

_____

_____

_____

_____

Talk to God at night about these obstacles and ask for His help. Turning it over to God doesn't mean you do nothing, but that you don't need to stress or worry. With God as your partner, you know you just need to do what you are able to do and leave the rest in His hands.

I have had some amazing experiences going to sleep with an obstacle or question and then waking at 4:30am with the answer. I know that between God and our subconscious working on the problem, ideas will come.

When you awake the next morning, before you look at any device, spend time thinking about your obstacle. Keep a prayer in your heart throughout the day and ask God to help you see or hear the solution. Write down any additional ideas or impressions below that may come to you. Then tweak it or find someone who can help you.

_____

_____

_____

_____

_____

Keep working and moving forward. If you find a closed door, trust that God has a better door for you to walk toward and keep your momentum going. You can also shift your focus to another mini goal until you the way opens. Pray and God will guide you.

END OF WEEK SUMMARY: WEEK __

Commit thy way unto the LORD; trust also in him; and he shall bring it to pass.

PSALM 37:5

God knows you and your situation perfectly. Remember the principle of grace as you review your week, and don't be hard on yourself.

What mini-goals did I accomplish this week?

___

___

___

___

What rewards did I enjoy?

___

___

___

___

What other things did I accomplish this week?

___

___

___

___

Are there any mini-goals that need to be modified or carried over to next week?

___

___

___

___

MY MIRACLES: Obstacles I have overcome this week and other ways I have seen God's hand.

Obstacles I have *"given to God"* for further illumination:

NOTES:

GOALS: WEEK ___

For thou art my rock and my fortress;
therefore for thy name's sake lead me, and guide me.

PSALM 31:3

My Inspired Resolution: DATE: _____

_____

MINI-GOALS – What I will accomplish this week + reward for each goal:

_____
_____
_____
_____

Now, **talk to God about it**. Tell Him about your weekly goals and ask for courage, faith, and patience to accomplish them.

Begin each morning with prayer. Tell God about your mini-goals and ask for the wisdom and determination to accomplish them. Schedule how you will work on one of your mini-goals that day and do it! Meditate and envision yourself accomplishing each goal and enjoying your reward.

Don't be discouraged if life throws curve balls at you during the day. Life happens. Give yourself grace and keep going. Learn more about how to overcome obstacles on the next page.

End every day with a prayer of thanks and a report of how you have done with your goals that day.

List any additional ideas or thoughts after your prayers below.

_____
_____
_____
_____

Be flexible enough to incorporate additional ideas into your weekly goals. This is how you learn to trust God and be spontaneous enough to walk through doors that come up mid-week.

OBSTACLES: WEEK __

In all these things we are more than conquerors through him that loved us.

ROMANS 8:37

During the week, take a few moments to evaluate this question:

What obstacles am I facing? _____

_____
_____
_____
_____

Talk to God at night about these obstacles and ask for His help. Turning it over to God doesn't mean you do nothing, but that you don't need to stress or worry. With God as your partner, you know you just need to do what you are able to do and leave the rest in His hands.

I have had some amazing experiences going to sleep with an obstacle or question and then waking at 4:30am with the answer. I know that between God and our subconscious working on the problem, ideas will come.

When you awake the next morning, before you look at any device, spend time thinking about your obstacle. Keep a prayer in your heart throughout the day and ask God to help you see or hear the solution. Write down any additional ideas or impressions below that may come to you. Then tweak it or find someone who can help you.

_____
_____
_____
_____
_____

Keep working and moving forward. If you find a closed door, trust that God has a better door for you to walk toward and keep your momentum going. You can also shift your focus to another mini goal until you the way opens. Pray and God will guide you.

END OF WEEK SUMMARY: WEEK __

Be ye strong therefore, and let not your hands be weak: for your work shall be rewarded.

2 CHRONICLES 15:7

God knows you and your situation perfectly. Remember the principle of grace as you review your week, and don't be hard on yourself.

What mini-goals did I accomplish this week?

_____
_____
_____
_____

What rewards did I enjoy?

_____
_____
_____
_____

What other things did I accomplish this week?

_____
_____
_____
_____

Are there any mini-goals that need to be modified or carried over to next week?

_____
_____
_____
_____

MY MIRACLES: Obstacles I have overcome this week and other ways I have seen God's hand.

_____
_____
_____
_____
_____

Obstacles I have *"given to God"* for further illumination:

_____
_____
_____
_____

NOTES: _____

_____
_____
_____
_____
_____
_____
_____
_____
_____
_____
_____
_____

GOALS: WEEK ___

Guide our feet into the way of peace.

LUKE 1:79

My Inspired Resolution: DATE: _____

_____

MINI-GOALS – What I will accomplish this week + reward for each goal:

_____

_____

_____

_____

Now, **talk to God about it**. Tell Him about your weekly goals and ask for courage, faith, and patience to accomplish them.

Begin each morning with prayer. Tell God about your mini-goals and ask for the wisdom and determination to accomplish them. Schedule how you will work on one of your mini-goals that day and do it! Meditate and envision yourself accomplishing each goal and enjoying your reward.

Don't be discouraged if life throws curve balls at you during the day. Life happens. Give yourself grace and keep going. Learn more about how to overcome obstacles on the next page.

End every day with a prayer of thanks and a report of how you have done with your goals that day.

List any additional ideas or thoughts after your prayers below.

_____

_____

_____

Be flexible enough to incorporate additional ideas into your weekly goals. This is how you learn to trust God and be spontaneous enough to walk through doors that come up mid-week.

OBSTACLES: WEEK __

Let us run with patience the race that is set before us.

HEBREWS 12:1

During the week, take a few moments to evaluate this question:

What obstacles am I facing? _____

_____

_____

_____

_____

Talk to God at night about these obstacles and ask for His help. Turning it over to God doesn't mean you do nothing, but that you don't need to stress or worry. With God as your partner, you know you just need to do what you are able to do and leave the rest in His hands.

I have had some amazing experiences going to sleep with an obstacle or question and then waking at 4:30am with the answer. I know that between God and our subconscious working on the problem, ideas will come.

When you awake the next morning, before you look at any device, spend time thinking about your obstacle. Keep a prayer in your heart throughout the day and ask God to help you see or hear the solution. Write down any additional ideas or impressions below that may come to you. Then tweak it or find someone who can help you.

_____

_____

_____

_____

_____

Keep working and moving forward. If you find a closed door, trust that God has a better door for you to walk toward and keep your momentum going. You can also shift your focus to another mini goal until you the way opens. Pray and God will guide you.

END OF WEEK SUMMARY: WEEK __

Delight thyself also in the LORD; and he shall give thee the desires of thine heart.

PSALM 37:4

God knows you and your situation perfectly. Remember the principle of grace as you review your week, and don't be hard on yourself.

What mini-goals did I accomplish this week?

_____
_____
_____
_____

What rewards did I enjoy?

_____
_____
_____
_____

What other things did I accomplish this week?

_____
_____
_____
_____

Are there any mini-goals that need to be modified or carried over to next week?

_____
_____
_____
_____

MY MIRACLES: Obstacles I have overcome this week and other ways I have seen God's hand.

_____
_____
_____
_____
_____

Obstacles I have *"given to God"* for further illumination:

_____
_____
_____
_____

NOTES: _____
_____
_____
_____
_____
_____
_____
_____
_____
_____
_____
_____
_____
_____

END OF MONTH SUMMARY

Cast not away therefore your confidence, ... For ye have need of patience, that, after ye have done the will of God, ye might receive the promise

HEBREWS 10:35-36

Fill in your data from this month's weekly goal sheets here.

What mini-goals did I accomplish this month?

_____
_____
_____
_____
_____
_____
_____
_____
_____
_____

What rewards did I enjoy?

_____
_____
_____
_____
_____

What other things did I accomplish this month?

_____
_____
_____
_____
_____
_____
_____
_____
_____
_____
_____

MY MIRACLES: Obstacles I have overcome this month and other ways I have seen God's hand:

_____
_____
_____
_____
_____
_____
_____
_____
_____
_____
_____
_____

How have I changed?

___

What mini-goals do I want to work on next month to keep moving forward?

___

Will you please email me at **tamarakandersonauthor@gmail.com** to tell me about your accomplishments this month? I'd love to rejoice with you in your success!

NOTES:

GOALS: WEEK ___

*I will instruct thee and teach thee in the way which thou shalt go:
I will guide thee with mine eye.*

PSALM 32:8

My Inspired Resolution: DATE: _____

_____

MINI-GOALS – What I will accomplish this week + reward for each goal:

_____

_____

_____

_____

Now, **talk to God about it**. Tell Him about your weekly goals and ask for courage, faith, and patience to accomplish them.

Begin each morning with prayer. Tell God about your mini-goals and ask for the wisdom and determination to accomplish them. Schedule how you will work on one of your mini-goals that day and do it! Meditate and envision yourself accomplishing each goal and enjoying your reward.

Don't be discouraged if life throws curve balls at you during the day. Life happens. Give yourself grace and keep going. Learn more about how to overcome obstacles on the next page.

End every day with a prayer of thanks and a report of how you have done with your goals that day.

List any additional ideas or thoughts after your prayers below.

_____

_____

_____

_____

Be flexible enough to incorporate additional ideas into your weekly goals. This is how you learn to trust God and be spontaneous enough to walk through doors that come up mid-week.

OBSTACLES: WEEK __

Fight the good fight of faith.

1 TIMOTHY 6:12

During the week, take a few moments to evaluate this question:

What obstacles am I facing? _____

_____

_____

_____

_____

Talk to God at night about these obstacles and ask for His help. Turning it over to God doesn't mean you do nothing, but that you don't need to stress or worry. With God as your partner, you know you just need to do what you are able to do and leave the rest in His hands.

I have had some amazing experiences going to sleep with an obstacle or question and then waking at 4:30am with the answer. I know that between God and our subconscious working on the problem, ideas will come.

When you awake the next morning, before you look at any device, spend time thinking about your obstacle. Keep a prayer in your heart throughout the day and ask God to help you see or hear the solution. Write down any additional ideas or impressions below that may come to you. Then tweak it or find someone who can help you.

_____

_____

_____

_____

Keep working and moving forward. If you find a closed door, trust that God has a better door for you to walk toward and keep your momentum going. You can also shift your focus to another mini goal until you the way opens. Pray and God will guide you.

END OF WEEK SUMMARY: WEEK __

But Jesus beheld them, and said unto them,
With men this is impossible; but with God all things are possible.

MATTHEW 19:26

God knows you and your situation perfectly. Remember the principle of grace as you review your week, and don't be hard on yourself.

What mini-goals did I accomplish this week?

_____
_____
_____
_____

What rewards did I enjoy?

_____
_____
_____
_____

What other things did I accomplish this week?

_____
_____
_____
_____

Are there any mini-goals that need to be modified or carried over to next week?

_____
_____
_____

MY MIRACLES: Obstacles I have overcome this week and other ways I have seen God's hand.

_____
_____
_____
_____
_____

Obstacles I have *"given to God"* for further illumination:

_____
_____
_____
_____

NOTES: _____

_____
_____
_____
_____
_____
_____
_____
_____
_____
_____
_____
_____
_____

GOALS: WEEK ___

And we know that all things work together for good to them that love God, to them who are the called according to his purpose.

ROMANS 8:28

My Inspired Resolution: DATE: _____

MINI-GOALS – What I will accomplish this week + reward for each goal:

_____

_____

_____

_____

Now, **talk to God about it**. Tell Him about your weekly goals and ask for courage, faith, and patience to accomplish them.

Begin each morning with prayer. Tell God about your mini-goals and ask for the wisdom and determination to accomplish them. Schedule how you will work on one of your mini-goals that day and do it! Meditate and envision yourself accomplishing each goal and enjoying your reward.

Don't be discouraged if life throws curve balls at you during the day. Life happens. Give yourself grace and keep going. Learn more about how to overcome obstacles on the next page.

End every day with a prayer of thanks and a report of how you have done with your goals that day.

List any additional ideas or thoughts after your prayers below.

_____

_____

_____

_____

Be flexible enough to incorporate additional ideas into your weekly goals. This is how you learn to trust God and be spontaneous enough to walk through doors that come up mid-week.

OBSTACLES: WEEK __

Ye are of God, little children, and have overcome them:
because greater is he that is in you, than he that is in the world.

1 JOHN 4:4

During the week, take a few moments to evaluate this question:

What obstacles am I facing? _____

_____

_____

_____

_____

Talk to God at night about these obstacles and ask for His help. Turning it over to God doesn't mean you do nothing, but that you don't need to stress or worry. With God as your partner, you know you just need to do what you are able to do and leave the rest in His hands.

I have had some amazing experiences going to sleep with an obstacle or question and then waking at 4:30am with the answer. I know that between God and our subconscious working on the problem, ideas will come.

When you awake the next morning, before you look at any device, spend time thinking about your obstacle. Keep a prayer in your heart throughout the day and ask God to help you see or hear the solution. Write down any additional ideas or impressions below that may come to you. Then tweak it or find someone who can help you.

_____

_____

_____

_____

_____

Keep working and moving forward. If you find a closed door, trust that God has a better door for you to walk toward and keep your momentum going. You can also shift your focus to another mini goal until you the way opens. Pray and God will guide you.

END OF WEEK SUMMARY: WEEK __

Be ye transformed by the renewing of your mind, that ye may prove what is that good, and acceptable, and perfect, will of God.

ROMANS 12:2

God knows you and your situation perfectly. Remember the principle of grace as you review your week, and don't be hard on yourself.

What mini-goals did I accomplish this week?

___

What rewards did I enjoy?

___

What other things did I accomplish this week?

___

Are there any mini-goals that need to be modified or carried over to next week?

___

MY MIRACLES: Obstacles I have overcome this week and other ways I have seen God's hand.

Obstacles I have *"given to God"* for further illumination:

NOTES:

GOALS: WEEK __

But they that wait upon the Lord shall renew their strength; they shall mount up with wings as eagles; they shall run, and not be weary; and they shall walk, and not faint.

ISAIAH 40:31

My Inspired Resolution: DATE: _____

MINI-GOALS – What I will accomplish this week + reward for each goal:

_____

_____

_____

_____

Now, **talk to God about it**. Tell Him about your weekly goals and ask for courage, faith, and patience to accomplish them.

Begin each morning with prayer. Tell God about your mini-goals and ask for the wisdom and determination to accomplish them. Schedule how you will work on one of your mini-goals that day and do it! Meditate and envision yourself accomplishing each goal and enjoying your reward.

Don't be discouraged if life throws curve balls at you during the day. Life happens. Give yourself grace and keep going. Learn more about how to overcome obstacles on the next page.

End every day with a prayer of thanks and a report of how you have done with your goals that day.

List any additional ideas or thoughts after your prayers below.

_____

_____

_____

_____

Be flexible enough to incorporate additional ideas into your weekly goals. This is how you learn to trust God and be spontaneous enough to walk through doors that come up mid-week.

OBSTACLES: WEEK __

O Lord, I beseech thee, send now prosperity.

PSALM 118:25

During the week, take a few moments to evaluate this question:

What obstacles am I facing? _____

_____
_____
_____
_____

Talk to God at night about these obstacles and ask for His help. Turning it over to God doesn't mean you do nothing, but that you don't need to stress or worry. With God as your partner, you know you just need to do what you are able to do and leave the rest in His hands.

I have had some amazing experiences going to sleep with an obstacle or question and then waking at 4:30am with the answer. I know that between God and our subconscious working on the problem, ideas will come.

When you awake the next morning, before you look at any device, spend time thinking about your obstacle. Keep a prayer in your heart throughout the day and ask God to help you see or hear the solution. Write down any additional ideas or impressions below that may come to you. Then tweak it or find someone who can help you.

_____
_____
_____
_____
_____

Keep working and moving forward. If you find a closed door, trust that God has a better door for you to walk toward and keep your momentum going. You can also shift your focus to another mini goal until you the way opens. Pray and God will guide you.

END OF WEEK SUMMARY: WEEK __

Whatsoever things are true, ... honest, ... just, ... pure, ... lovely, ... good report; if there be any virtue, and if there be any praise, think on these things.

PHILIPPIANS 4:8

God knows you and your situation perfectly. Remember the principle of grace as you review your week, and don't be hard on yourself.

What mini-goals did I accomplish this week?

___

What rewards did I enjoy?

___

What other things did I accomplish this week?

___

Are there any mini-goals that need to be modified or carried over to next week?

___

MY MIRACLES: Obstacles I have overcome this week and other ways I have seen God's hand.

_____
_____
_____
_____
_____

Obstacles I have *"given to God"* for further illumination:

_____
_____
_____
_____

NOTES: _____
_____
_____
_____
_____
_____
_____
_____
_____
_____
_____
_____
_____

GOALS: WEEK ___

Great is thy faithfulness. The Lord is my portion, saith my soul; therefore I will hope in him.
LAMENTATIONS 3:23-24

My Inspired Resolution: DATE: _____

_____

MINI-GOALS – What I will accomplish this week + reward for each goal:

_____

_____

_____

_____

Now, **talk to God about it.** Tell Him about your weekly goals and ask for courage, faith, and patience to accomplish them.

Begin each morning with prayer. Tell God about your mini-goals and ask for the wisdom and determination to accomplish them. Schedule how you will work on one of your mini-goals that day and do it! Meditate and envision yourself accomplishing each goal and enjoying your reward.

Don't be discouraged if life throws curve balls at you during the day. Life happens. Give yourself grace and keep going. Learn more about how to overcome obstacles on the next page.

End every day with a prayer of thanks and a report of how you have done with your goals that day.

List any additional ideas or thoughts after your prayers below.

_____

_____

_____

Be flexible enough to incorporate additional ideas into your weekly goals. This is how you learn to trust God and be spontaneous enough to walk through doors that come up mid-week.

OBSTACLES: WEEK __

Thou shalt preserve me from trouble; thou shalt compass me about with songs of deliverance.

PSALM 32:7

During the week, take a few moments to evaluate this question:

What obstacles am I facing? _____

_____

_____

_____

_____

Talk to God at night about these obstacles and ask for His help. Turning it over to God doesn't mean you do nothing, but that you don't need to stress or worry. With God as your partner, you know you just need to do what you are able to do and leave the rest in His hands.

I have had some amazing experiences going to sleep with an obstacle or question and then waking at 4:30am with the answer. I know that between God and our subconscious working on the problem, ideas will come.

When you awake the next morning, before you look at any device, spend time thinking about your obstacle. Keep a prayer in your heart throughout the day and ask God to help you see or hear the solution. Write down any additional ideas or impressions below that may come to you. Then tweak it or find someone who can help you.

_____

_____

_____

_____

_____

Keep working and moving forward. If you find a closed door, trust that God has a better door for you to walk toward and keep your momentum going. You can also shift your focus to another mini goal until you the way opens. Pray and God will guide you.

END OF WEEK SUMMARY: WEEK __

Jesus saith unto them, My meat is to do the will of him that sent me, and to finish his work.

JOHN 4:34

God knows you and your situation perfectly. Remember the principle of grace as you review your week, and don't be hard on yourself.

What mini-goals did I accomplish this week?

What rewards did I enjoy?

What other things did I accomplish this week?

Are there any mini-goals that need to be modified or carried over to next week?

MY MIRACLES: Obstacles I have overcome this week and other ways I have seen God's hand.

_____
_____
_____
_____
_____

Obstacles I have *"given to God"* for further illumination:

_____
_____
_____
_____

NOTES: _____
_____
_____
_____
_____
_____
_____
_____
_____
_____
_____
_____
_____

GOALS: WEEK ___

It is good that a man should both hope and quietly wait for the salvation of the Lord.

LAMENTATIONS 3:26

My Inspired Resolution: DATE: _____

_____

MINI-GOALS – What I will accomplish this week + reward for each goal:

_____

_____

_____

_____

Now, **talk to God about it**. Tell Him about your weekly goals and ask for courage, faith, and patience to accomplish them.

Begin each morning with prayer. Tell God about your mini-goals and ask for the wisdom and determination to accomplish them. Schedule how you will work on one of your mini-goals that day and do it! Meditate and envision yourself accomplishing each goal and enjoying your reward.

Don't be discouraged if life throws curve balls at you during the day. Life happens. Give yourself grace and keep going. Learn more about how to overcome obstacles on the next page.

End every day with a prayer of thanks and a report of how you have done with your goals that day.

List any additional ideas or thoughts after your prayers below.

_____

_____

_____

_____

Be flexible enough to incorporate additional ideas into your weekly goals. This is how you learn to trust God and be spontaneous enough to walk through doors that come up mid-week.

OBSTACLES: WEEK __

And ye shall seek me, and find me, when ye shall search for me with all your heart.

JEREMIAH 29:13

During the week, take a few moments to evaluate this question:

What obstacles am I facing? _____

_____

_____

_____

_____

Talk to God at night about these obstacles and ask for His help. Turning it over to God doesn't mean you do nothing, but that you don't need to stress or worry. With God as your partner, you know you just need to do what you are able to do and leave the rest in His hands.

I have had some amazing experiences going to sleep with an obstacle or question and then waking at 4:30am with the answer. I know that between God and our subconscious working on the problem, ideas will come.

When you awake the next morning, before you look at any device, spend time thinking about your obstacle. Keep a prayer in your heart throughout the day and ask God to help you see or hear the solution. Write down any additional ideas or impressions below that may come to you. Then tweak it or find someone who can help you.

_____

_____

_____

_____

_____

Keep working and moving forward. If you find a closed door, trust that God has a better door for you to walk toward and keep your momentum going. You can also shift your focus to another mini goal until you the way opens. Pray and God will guide you.

END OF WEEK SUMMARY: WEEK __

And all things, whatsoever ye shall ask in prayer, believing, ye shall receive.

MATTHEW 21:22

God knows you and your situation perfectly. Remember the principle of grace as you review your week, and don't be hard on yourself.

What mini-goals did I accomplish this week?

_____
_____
_____
_____

What rewards did I enjoy?

_____
_____
_____
_____

What other things did I accomplish this week?

_____
_____
_____
_____

Are there any mini-goals that need to be modified or carried over to next week?

_____
_____
_____
_____

MY MIRACLES: Obstacles I have overcome this week and other ways I have seen God's hand.

_____
_____
_____
_____
_____

Obstacles I have *"given to God"* for further illumination:

_____
_____
_____
_____

NOTES: _____

_____
_____
_____
_____
_____
_____
_____
_____
_____
_____
_____
_____
_____
_____

END OF MONTH SUMMARY

The desire accomplished is sweet to the soul.

PROVERBS 13:19

Fill in your data from this month's weekly goal sheets here.

What mini-goals did I accomplish this month?

_____
_____
_____
_____
_____
_____
_____
_____
_____
_____
_____

What rewards did I enjoy?

_____
_____
_____
_____
_____

What other things did I accomplish this month?

MY MIRACLES: Obstacles I have overcome this month and other ways I have seen God's hand:

How have I changed?

___

What mini-goals do I want to work on next month to keep moving forward?

___

Will you please email me at **tamarakandersonauthor@gmail.com** to tell me about your accomplishments this month? I'd love to rejoice with you in your success!

NOTES:

END OF FIRST THIRD QUARTER SUMMARY

For I know the thoughts that I think toward you, saith the LORD, thoughts of peace, and not of evil, to give you an expected end.

JEREMIAH 29:11

Fill in your data from this quarter's monthly goal sheets here.

DATE: _____

What mini-goals did I accomplish this during the last three months?

What rewards did I enjoy?

What other things did I accomoplish?

MY MIRACLES: Obstacles I have overcome during the past 3 months and other ways I have seen God's hand:

How have I changed?

What mini-goals do I want to work on during the next quarter to keep moving forward?

FOURTH QUARTER
Goal Worksheets

GOALS: WEEK ___

Trust in the Lord, and do good.

PSALM 37:3

My Inspired Resolution: DATE: _____

_____

MINI-GOALS – What I will accomplish this week + reward for each goal:

_____

_____

_____

_____

Now, **talk to God about it**. Tell Him about your weekly goals and ask for courage, faith, and patience to accomplish them.

Begin each morning with prayer. Tell God about your mini-goals and ask for the wisdom and determination to accomplish them. Schedule how you will work on one of your mini-goals that day and do it! Meditate and envision yourself accomplishing each goal and enjoying your reward.

Don't be discouraged if life throws curve balls at you during the day. Life happens. Give yourself grace and keep going. Learn more about how to overcome obstacles on the next page.

End every day with a prayer of thanks and a report of how you have done with your goals that day.

List any additional ideas or thoughts after your prayers below.

_____

_____

_____

Be flexible enough to incorporate additional ideas into your weekly goals. This is how you learn to trust God and be spontaneous enough to walk through doors that come up mid-week.

OBSTACLES: WEEK __

For this thing I besought the Lord thrice, that it might depart from me.

2 CORINTHIANS 12:8

During the week, take a few moments to evaluate this question:

What obstacles am I facing? _____

_____

_____

_____

_____

Talk to God at night about these obstacles and ask for His help. Turning it over to God doesn't mean you do nothing, but that you don't need to stress or worry. With God as your partner, you know you just need to do what you are able to do and leave the rest in His hands.

I have had some amazing experiences going to sleep with an obstacle or question and then waking at 4:30am with the answer. I know that between God and our subconscious working on the problem, ideas will come.

When you awake the next morning, before you look at any device, spend time thinking about your obstacle. Keep a prayer in your heart throughout the day and ask God to help you see or hear the solution. Write down any additional ideas or impressions below that may come to you. Then tweak it or find someone who can help you.

_____

_____

_____

_____

_____

Keep working and moving forward. If you find a closed door, trust that God has a better door for you to walk toward and keep your momentum going. You can also shift your focus to another mini goal until you the way opens. Pray and God will guide you.

END OF WEEK SUMMARY: WEEK __

But SEEK YE FIRST THE KINGDOM OF GOD, *and his righteousness; and all these things shall be added unto you.*

MATTHEW 6:33

God knows you and your situation perfectly. Remember the principle of grace as you review your week, and don't be hard on yourself.

What mini-goals did I accomplish this week?

_____
_____
_____
_____

What rewards did I enjoy?

_____
_____
_____
_____

What other things did I accomplish this week?

_____
_____
_____
_____

Are there any mini-goals that need to be modified or carried over to next week?

_____
_____
_____

MY MIRACLES: Obstacles I have overcome this week and other ways I have seen God's hand.

Obstacles I have *"given to God"* for further illumination:

NOTES:

GOALS: WEEK ___

I can do all things through Christ which strengtheneth me.

PHILIPPIANS 4:13

My Inspired Resolution: DATE: _____

_____

MINI-GOALS – What I will accomplish this week + reward for each goal:

_____

_____

_____

_____

Now, **talk to God about it**. Tell Him about your weekly goals and ask for courage, faith, and patience to accomplish them.

Begin each morning with prayer. Tell God about your mini-goals and ask for the wisdom and determination to accomplish them. Schedule how you will work on one of your mini-goals that day and do it! Meditate and envision yourself accomplishing each goal and enjoying your reward.

Don't be discouraged if life throws curve balls at you during the day. Life happens. Give yourself grace and keep going. Learn more about how to overcome obstacles on the next page.

End every day with a prayer of thanks and a report of how you have done with your goals that day.

List any additional ideas or thoughts after your prayers below.

_____

_____

_____

Be flexible enough to incorporate additional ideas into your weekly goals. This is how you learn to trust God and be spontaneous enough to walk through doors that come up mid-week.

OBSTACLES: WEEK __

We glory in tribulations also: knowing that tribulation worketh patience.

ROMANS 5:3

During the week, take a few moments to evaluate this question:

What obstacles am I facing? _____

_____
_____
_____
_____

Talk to God at night about these obstacles and ask for His help. Turning it over to God doesn't mean you do nothing, but that you don't need to stress or worry. With God as your partner, you know you just need to do what you are able to do and leave the rest in His hands.

I have had some amazing experiences going to sleep with an obstacle or question and then waking at 4:30am with the answer. I know that between God and our subconscious working on the problem, ideas will come.

When you awake the next morning, before you look at any device, spend time thinking about your obstacle. Keep a prayer in your heart throughout the day and ask God to help you see or hear the solution. Write down any additional ideas or impressions below that may come to you. Then tweak it or find someone who can help you.

_____
_____
_____
_____
_____

Keep working and moving forward. If you find a closed door, trust that God has a better door for you to walk toward and keep your momentum going. You can also shift your focus to another mini goal until you the way opens. Pray and God will guide you.

END OF WEEK SUMMARY: WEEK __

Know ye not that they which run in a race run all, but one receiveth the prize? So run, that ye may obtain.

1 CORINTHIANS 9:24

God knows you and your situation perfectly. Remember the principle of grace as you review your week, and don't be hard on yourself.

What mini-goals did I accomplish this week?

___

What rewards did I enjoy?

___

What other things did I accomplish this week?

___

Are there any mini-goals that need to be modified or carried over to next week?

___

MY MIRACLES: Obstacles I have overcome this week and other ways I have seen God's hand.

_____
_____
_____
_____
_____

Obstacles I have *"given to God"* for further illumination:

_____
_____
_____
_____

NOTES: _____
_____
_____
_____
_____
_____
_____
_____
_____
_____
_____
_____
_____
_____

GOALS: WEEK ___

All that the Lord hath said will we do.

EXODUS 24:7

My Inspired Resolution: DATE: _____

MINI-GOALS – What I will accomplish this week + reward for each goal:

_____

_____

_____

_____

Now, **talk to God about it**. Tell Him about your weekly goals and ask for courage, faith, and patience to accomplish them.

Begin each morning with prayer. Tell God about your mini-goals and ask for the wisdom and determination to accomplish them. Schedule how you will work on one of your mini-goals that day and do it! Meditate and envision yourself accomplishing each goal and enjoying your reward.

Don't be discouraged if life throws curve balls at you during the day. Life happens. Give yourself grace and keep going. Learn more about how to overcome obstacles on the next page.

End every day with a prayer of thanks and a report of how you have done with your goals that day.

List any additional ideas or thoughts after your prayers below.

_____

_____

_____

Be flexible enough to incorporate additional ideas into your weekly goals. This is how you learn to trust God and be spontaneous enough to walk through doors that come up mid-week.

OBSTACLES: WEEK __

If ye have faith as a grain of mustard seed, ye shall say unto this mountain, Remove hence to yonder place; and it shall remove; and nothing shall be impossible unto you.

MATTHEW 17:20

During the week, take a few moments to evaluate this question:

What obstacles am I facing? _____

_____

_____

_____

_____

Talk to God at night about these obstacles and ask for His help. Turning it over to God doesn't mean you do nothing, but that you don't need to stress or worry. With God as your partner, you know you just need to do what you are able to do and leave the rest in His hands.

I have had some amazing experiences going to sleep with an obstacle or question and then waking at 4:30am with the answer. I know that between God and our subconscious working on the problem, ideas will come.

When you awake the next morning, before you look at any device, spend time thinking about your obstacle. Keep a prayer in your heart throughout the day and ask God to help you see or hear the solution. Write down any additional ideas or impressions below that may come to you. Then tweak it or find someone who can help you.

_____

_____

_____

_____

_____

Keep working and moving forward. If you find a closed door, trust that God has a better door for you to walk toward and keep your momentum going. You can also shift your focus to another mini goal until you the way opens. Pray and God will guide you.

END OF WEEK SUMMARY: WEEK __

Fear thou not; for I am with thee: be not dismayed; for I am thy God: I will strengthen thee; yea, I will help thee; yea, I will uphold thee with the right hand of my righteousness.

ISAIAH 41:10

God knows you and your situation perfectly. Remember the principle of grace as you review your week, and don't be hard on yourself.

What mini-goals did I accomplish this week?

_____
_____
_____
_____

What rewards did I enjoy?

_____
_____
_____
_____

What other things did I accomplish this week?

_____
_____
_____
_____

Are there any mini-goals that need to be modified or carried over to next week?

_____
_____
_____

MY MIRACLES: Obstacles I have overcome this week and other ways I have seen God's hand.

_____
_____
_____
_____
_____

Obstacles I have *"given to God"* for further illumination:

_____
_____
_____
_____

NOTES: _____
_____
_____
_____
_____
_____
_____
_____
_____
_____
_____
_____
_____

GOALS: WEEK ___

Trust in the Lord with all thine heart; and lean not unto thine own understanding. In all thy ways acknowledge Him, and He shall direct thy paths.

PROVERBS 3:5-6

My Inspired Resolution: DATE: _____

_____

MINI-GOALS – What I will accomplish this week + reward for each goal:

_____

_____

_____

_____

Now, **talk to God about it**. Tell Him about your weekly goals and ask for courage, faith, and patience to accomplish them.

Begin each morning with prayer. Tell God about your mini-goals and ask for the wisdom and determination to accomplish them. Schedule how you will work on one of your mini-goals that day and do it! Meditate and envision yourself accomplishing each goal and enjoying your reward.

Don't be discouraged if life throws curve balls at you during the day. Life happens. Give yourself grace and keep going. Learn more about how to overcome obstacles on the next page.

End every day with a prayer of thanks and a report of how you have done with your goals that day.

List any additional ideas or thoughts after your prayers below.

_____

_____

_____

_____

Be flexible enough to incorporate additional ideas into your weekly goals. This is how you learn to trust God and be spontaneous enough to walk through doors that come up mid-week.

OBSTACLES: WEEK __

Prepare the way, take up the stumblingblock out of the way of my people.

ISAIAH 57:14

During the week, take a few moments to evaluate this question:

What obstacles am I facing? _____

_____

_____

_____

_____

Talk to God at night about these obstacles and ask for His help. Turning it over to God doesn't mean you do nothing, but that you don't need to stress or worry. With God as your partner, you know you just need to do what you are able to do and leave the rest in His hands.

I have had some amazing experiences going to sleep with an obstacle or question and then waking at 4:30am with the answer. I know that between God and our subconscious working on the problem, ideas will come.

When you awake the next morning, before you look at any device, spend time thinking about your obstacle. Keep a prayer in your heart throughout the day and ask God to help you see or hear the solution. Write down any additional ideas or impressions below that may come to you. Then tweak it or find someone who can help you.

_____

_____

_____

_____

_____

Keep working and moving forward. If you find a closed door, trust that God has a better door for you to walk toward and keep your momentum going. You can also shift your focus to another mini goal until you the way opens. Pray and God will guide you.

END OF WEEK SUMMARY: WEEK __

Commit thy works unto the Lord, and thy thoughts shall be established.

PROVERBS 16:3

God knows you and your situation perfectly. Remember the principle of grace as you review your week, and don't be hard on yourself.

What mini-goals did I accomplish this week?

_____
_____
_____
_____

What rewards did I enjoy?

_____
_____
_____
_____

What other things did I accomplish this week?

_____
_____
_____
_____

Are there any mini-goals that need to be modified or carried over to next week?

_____
_____
_____
_____

MY MIRACLES: Obstacles I have overcome this week and other ways I have seen God's hand.

_____
_____
_____
_____
_____
_____

Obstacles I have *"given to God"* for further illumination:

_____
_____
_____
_____
_____

NOTES: _____

_____
_____
_____
_____
_____
_____
_____
_____
_____
_____
_____
_____
_____

GOALS: WEEK ___

For God hath not given us the spirit of fear; but of power, and of love, and of a sound mind."
2 TIMOTHY 1:7

My Inspired Resolution: DATE: _____

_____

MINI-GOALS – What I will accomplish this week + reward for each goal:

_____

_____

_____

_____

Now, **talk to God about it**. Tell Him about your weekly goals and ask for courage, faith, and patience to accomplish them.

Begin each morning with prayer. Tell God about your mini-goals and ask for the wisdom and determination to accomplish them. Schedule how you will work on one of your mini-goals that day and do it! Meditate and envision yourself accomplishing each goal and enjoying your reward.

Don't be discouraged if life throws curve balls at you during the day. Life happens. Give yourself grace and keep going. Learn more about how to overcome obstacles on the next page.

End every day with a prayer of thanks and a report of how you have done with your goals that day.

List any additional ideas or thoughts after your prayers below.

_____

_____

_____

_____

Be flexible enough to incorporate additional ideas into your weekly goals. This is how you learn to trust God and be spontaneous enough to walk through doors that come up mid-week.

OBSTACLES: WEEK __

The LORD shall fight for you, and ye shall hold your peace.

EXODUS 14:14

During the week, take a few moments to evaluate this question:

What obstacles am I facing? _____

_____

_____

_____

_____

Talk to God at night about these obstacles and ask for His help. Turning it over to God doesn't mean you do nothing, but that you don't need to stress or worry. With God as your partner, you know you just need to do what you are able to do and leave the rest in His hands.

I have had some amazing experiences going to sleep with an obstacle or question and then waking at 4:30am with the answer. I know that between God and our subconscious working on the problem, ideas will come.

When you awake the next morning, before you look at any device, spend time thinking about your obstacle. Keep a prayer in your heart throughout the day and ask God to help you see or hear the solution. Write down any additional ideas or impressions below that may come to you. Then tweak it or find someone who can help you.

_____

_____

_____

_____

_____

Keep working and moving forward. If you find a closed door, trust that God has a better door for you to walk toward and keep your momentum going. You can also shift your focus to another mini goal until you the way opens. Pray and God will guide you.

END OF WEEK SUMMARY: WEEK __

A man's heart deviseth his way: but the Lord directeth his steps.

PROVERBS 16:9

God knows you and your situation perfectly. Remember the principle of grace as you review your week, and don't be hard on yourself.

What mini-goals did I accomplish this week?

_____
_____
_____
_____

What rewards did I enjoy?

_____
_____
_____
_____

What other things did I accomplish this week?

_____
_____
_____
_____

Are there any mini-goals that need to be modified or carried over to next week?

_____
_____
_____
_____

MY MIRACLES: Obstacles I have overcome this week and other ways I have seen God's hand.

Obstacles I have *"given to God"* for further illumination:

NOTES:

END OF MONTH SUMMARY

In all thy ways acknowledge him, and he shall direct thy paths.

PROVERBS 3:6

Fill in your data from this month's weekly goal sheets here.

What mini-goals did I accomplish this month?

_____
_____
_____
_____
_____
_____
_____
_____
_____
_____

What rewards did I enjoy?

_____
_____
_____
_____
_____

What other things did I accomplish this month?

MY MIRACLES: Obstacles I have overcome this month and other ways I have seen God's hand:

How have I changed?

What mini-goals do I want to work on next month to keep moving forward?

Will you please email me at **tamarakandersonauthor@gmail.com** to tell me about your accomplishments this month? I'd love to rejoice with you in your success!

NOTES:

GOALS: WEEK ___

Shew me thy ways, O Lord; teach me thy paths.

PSALM 25:4

My Inspired Resolution: DATE: _____

MINI-GOALS – What I will accomplish this week + reward for each goal:

Now, **talk to God about it**. Tell Him about your weekly goals and ask for courage, faith, and patience to accomplish them.

Begin each morning with prayer. Tell God about your mini-goals and ask for the wisdom and determination to accomplish them. Schedule how you will work on one of your mini-goals that day and do it! Meditate and envision yourself accomplishing each goal and enjoying your reward.

Don't be discouraged if life throws curve balls at you during the day. Life happens. Give yourself grace and keep going. Learn more about how to overcome obstacles on the next page.

End every day with a prayer of thanks and a report of how you have done with your goals that day.

List any additional ideas or thoughts after your prayers below.

Be flexible enough to incorporate additional ideas into your weekly goals. This is how you learn to trust God and be spontaneous enough to walk through doors that come up mid-week.

OBSTACLES: WEEK __

In the world ye shall have tribulation: but be of good cheer; I have overcome the world.

JOHN 16:33

During the week, take a few moments to evaluate this question:

What obstacles am I facing? _____

_____
_____
_____
_____

Talk to God at night about these obstacles and ask for His help. Turning it over to God doesn't mean you do nothing, but that you don't need to stress or worry. With God as your partner, you know you just need to do what you are able to do and leave the rest in His hands.

I have had some amazing experiences going to sleep with an obstacle or question and then waking at 4:30am with the answer. I know that between God and our subconscious working on the problem, ideas will come.

When you awake the next morning, before you look at any device, spend time thinking about your obstacle. Keep a prayer in your heart throughout the day and ask God to help you see or hear the solution. Write down any additional ideas or impressions below that may come to you. Then tweak it or find someone who can help you.

_____
_____
_____
_____
_____

Keep working and moving forward. If you find a closed door, trust that God has a better door for you to walk toward and keep your momentum going. You can also shift your focus to another mini goal until you the way opens. Pray and God will guide you.

END OF WEEK SUMMARY: WEEK __

Where there is no vision, the people perish.

PROVERBS 29:18

God knows you and your situation perfectly. Remember the principle of grace as you review your week, and don't be hard on yourself.

What mini-goals did I accomplish this week?

_____
_____
_____
_____

What rewards did I enjoy?

_____
_____
_____
_____

What other things did I accomplish this week?

_____
_____
_____
_____

Are there any mini-goals that need to be modified or carried over to next week?

_____
_____
_____
_____

MY MIRACLES: Obstacles I have overcome this week and other ways I have seen God's hand.

Obstacles I have *"given to God"* for further illumination:

NOTES:

GOALS: WEEK ___

The Lord is my shepherd. I shall not want . . . He leadeth me in the paths of righteousness . . . I will fear no evil: for thou art with me.

PSALM 23: 1, 3, 4

My Inspired Resolution: DATE: _____

_____

MINI-GOALS – What I will accomplish this week + reward for each goal:

_____

_____

_____

Now, **talk to God about it**. Tell Him about your weekly goals and ask for courage, faith, and patience to accomplish them.

Begin each morning with prayer. Tell God about your mini-goals and ask for the wisdom and determination to accomplish them. Schedule how you will work on one of your mini-goals that day and do it! Meditate and envision yourself accomplishing each goal and enjoying your reward.

Don't be discouraged if life throws curve balls at you during the day. Life happens. Give yourself grace and keep going. Learn more about how to overcome obstacles on the next page.

End every day with a prayer of thanks and a report of how you have done with your goals that day.

List any additional ideas or thoughts after your prayers below.

_____

_____

_____

Be flexible enough to incorporate additional ideas into your weekly goals. This is how you learn to trust God and be spontaneous enough to walk through doors that come up mid-week.

OBSTACLES: WEEK __

Be not overcome of evil, but overcome evil with good.

ROMANS 12:21

During the week, take a few moments to evaluate this question:

What obstacles am I facing? _____

_____
_____
_____
_____

Talk to God at night about these obstacles and ask for His help. Turning it over to God doesn't mean you do nothing, but that you don't need to stress or worry. With God as your partner, you know you just need to do what you are able to do and leave the rest in His hands.

I have had some amazing experiences going to sleep with an obstacle or question and then waking at 4:30am with the answer. I know that between God and our subconscious working on the problem, ideas will come.

When you awake the next morning, before you look at any device, spend time thinking about your obstacle. Keep a prayer in your heart throughout the day and ask God to help you see or hear the solution. Write down any additional ideas or impressions below that may come to you. Then tweak it or find someone who can help you.

_____
_____
_____
_____
_____

Keep working and moving forward. If you find a closed door, trust that God has a better door for you to walk toward and keep your momentum going. You can also shift your focus to another mini goal until you the way opens. Pray and God will guide you.

END OF WEEK SUMMARY: WEEK __

I press toward the mark.

PHILIPPIANS 3:14

God knows you and your situation perfectly. Remember the principle of grace as you review your week, and don't be hard on yourself.

What mini-goals did I accomplish this week?

_____
_____
_____
_____

What rewards did I enjoy?

_____
_____
_____
_____

What other things did I accomplish this week?

_____
_____
_____
_____

Are there any mini-goals that need to be modified or carried over to next week?

_____
_____
_____
_____

MY MIRACLES: Obstacles I have overcome this week and other ways I have seen God's hand.

Obstacles I have *"given to God"* for further illumination:

NOTES:

GOALS: WEEK ___

For this God is our God for ever and ever: He will be our guide even unto death.

PSALM 48:14

My Inspired Resolution: DATE: _____

MINI-GOALS – What I will accomplish this week + reward for each goal:

Now, **talk to God about it.** Tell Him about your weekly goals and ask for courage, faith, and patience to accomplish them.

Begin each morning with prayer. Tell God about your mini-goals and ask for the wisdom and determination to accomplish them. Schedule how you will work on one of your mini-goals that day and do it! Meditate and envision yourself accomplishing each goal and enjoying your reward.

Don't be discouraged if life throws curve balls at you during the day. Life happens. Give yourself grace and keep going. Learn more about how to overcome obstacles on the next page.

End every day with a prayer of thanks and a report of how you have done with your goals that day.

List any additional ideas or thoughts after your prayers below.

Be flexible enough to incorporate additional ideas into your weekly goals. This is how you learn to trust God and be spontaneous enough to walk through doors that come up mid-week.

OBSTACLES: WEEK __

Thanks be to God, which giveth us the victory through our Lord Jesus Christ.

1 CORINTHIANS 15:57

During the week, take a few moments to evaluate this question:

What obstacles am I facing? _____

_____

_____

_____

_____

Talk to God at night about these obstacles and ask for His help. Turning it over to God doesn't mean you do nothing, but that you don't need to stress or worry. With God as your partner, you know you just need to do what you are able to do and leave the rest in His hands.

I have had some amazing experiences going to sleep with an obstacle or question and then waking at 4:30am with the answer. I know that between God and our subconscious working on the problem, ideas will come.

When you awake the next morning, before you look at any device, spend time thinking about your obstacle. Keep a prayer in your heart throughout the day and ask God to help you see or hear the solution. Write down any additional ideas or impressions below that may come to you. Then tweak it or find someone who can help you.

_____

_____

_____

_____

_____

Keep working and moving forward. If you find a closed door, trust that God has a better door for you to walk toward and keep your momentum going. You can also shift your focus to another mini goal until you the way opens. Pray and God will guide you.

END OF WEEK SUMMARY: WEEK __

Commit thy way unto the LORD; trust also in him; and he shall bring it to pass.

PSALM 37:5

God knows you and your situation perfectly. Remember the principle of grace as you review your week, and don't be hard on yourself.

What mini-goals did I accomplish this week?

_____
_____
_____
_____

What rewards did I enjoy?

_____
_____
_____
_____

What other things did I accomplish this week?

_____
_____
_____

Are there any mini-goals that need to be modified or carried over to next week?

_____
_____
_____
_____

MY MIRACLES: Obstacles I have overcome this week and other ways I have seen God's hand.

_____
_____
_____
_____
_____
_____

Obstacles I have *"given to God"* for further illumination:

_____
_____
_____
_____
_____

NOTES: _____
_____
_____
_____
_____
_____
_____
_____
_____
_____
_____
_____
_____

GOALS: WEEK ___

For thou art my rock and my fortress;
therefore for thy name's sake lead me, and guide me.

PSALM 31:3

My Inspired Resolution: DATE: _____

MINI-GOALS – What I will accomplish this week + reward for each goal:

Now, **talk to God about it**. Tell Him about your weekly goals and ask for courage, faith, and patience to accomplish them.

Begin each morning with prayer. Tell God about your mini-goals and ask for the wisdom and determination to accomplish them. Schedule how you will work on one of your mini-goals that day and do it! Meditate and envision yourself accomplishing each goal and enjoying your reward.

Don't be discouraged if life throws curve balls at you during the day. Life happens. Give yourself grace and keep going. Learn more about how to overcome obstacles on the next page.

End every day with a prayer of thanks and a report of how you have done with your goals that day.

List any additional ideas or thoughts after your prayers below.

Be flexible enough to incorporate additional ideas into your weekly goals. This is how you learn to trust God and be spontaneous enough to walk through doors that come up mid-week.

OBSTACLES: WEEK __

In all these things we are more than conquerors through him that loved us.

ROMANS 8:37

During the week, take a few moments to evaluate this question:

What obstacles am I facing? _____

_____
_____
_____
_____

Talk to God at night about these obstacles and ask for His help. Turning it over to God doesn't mean you do nothing, but that you don't need to stress or worry. With God as your partner, you know you just need to do what you are able to do and leave the rest in His hands.

I have had some amazing experiences going to sleep with an obstacle or question and then waking at 4:30am with the answer. I know that between God and our subconscious working on the problem, ideas will come.

When you awake the next morning, before you look at any device, spend time thinking about your obstacle. Keep a prayer in your heart throughout the day and ask God to help you see or hear the solution. Write down any additional ideas or impressions below that may come to you. Then tweak it or find someone who can help you.

_____
_____
_____
_____
_____
_____

Keep working and moving forward. If you find a closed door, trust that God has a better door for you to walk toward and keep your momentum going. You can also shift your focus to another mini goal until you the way opens. Pray and God will guide you.

END OF WEEK SUMMARY: WEEK __

Be ye strong therefore, and let not your hands be weak: for your work shall be rewarded.

2 CHRONICLES 15:7

God knows you and your situation perfectly. Remember the principle of grace as you review your week, and don't be hard on yourself.

What mini-goals did I accomplish this week?

_____
_____
_____
_____

What rewards did I enjoy?

_____
_____
_____
_____

What other things did I accomplish this week?

_____
_____
_____
_____

Are there any mini-goals that need to be modified or carried over to next week?

_____
_____
_____
_____

MY MIRACLES: Obstacles I have overcome this week and other ways I have seen God's hand.

_____
_____
_____
_____
_____

Obstacles I have *"given to God"* for further illumination:

_____
_____
_____
_____

NOTES: _____

_____
_____
_____
_____
_____
_____
_____
_____
_____
_____
_____
_____

GOALS: WEEK ___

Guide our feet into the way of peace.

LUKE 1:79

My Inspired Resolution: DATE: _____

_____

MINI-GOALS – What I will accomplish this week + reward for each goal:

_____

_____

_____

_____

Now, **talk to God about it**. Tell Him about your weekly goals and ask for courage, faith, and patience to accomplish them.

Begin each morning with prayer. Tell God about your mini-goals and ask for the wisdom and determination to accomplish them. Schedule how you will work on one of your mini-goals that day and do it! Meditate and envision yourself accomplishing each goal and enjoying your reward.

Don't be discouraged if life throws curve balls at you during the day. Life happens. Give yourself grace and keep going. Learn more about how to overcome obstacles on the next page.

End every day with a prayer of thanks and a report of how you have done with your goals that day.

List any additional ideas or thoughts after your prayers below.

_____

_____

_____

Be flexible enough to incorporate additional ideas into your weekly goals. This is how you learn to trust God and be spontaneous enough to walk through doors that come up mid-week.

OBSTACLES: WEEK __

Let us run with patience the race that is set before us.

HEBREWS 12:1

During the week, take a few moments to evaluate this question:

What obstacles am I facing? _____

_____
_____
_____
_____

Talk to God at night about these obstacles and ask for His help. Turning it over to God doesn't mean you do nothing, but that you don't need to stress or worry. With God as your partner, you know you just need to do what you are able to do and leave the rest in His hands.

I have had some amazing experiences going to sleep with an obstacle or question and then waking at 4:30am with the answer. I know that between God and our subconscious working on the problem, ideas will come.

When you awake the next morning, before you look at any device, spend time thinking about your obstacle. Keep a prayer in your heart throughout the day and ask God to help you see or hear the solution. Write down any additional ideas or impressions below that may come to you. Then tweak it or find someone who can help you.

_____
_____
_____
_____
_____

Keep working and moving forward. If you find a closed door, trust that God has a better door for you to walk toward and keep your momentum going. You can also shift your focus to another mini goal until you the way opens. Pray and God will guide you.

END OF WEEK SUMMARY: WEEK ___

Delight thyself also in the LORD; and he shall give thee the desires of thine heart.

PSALM 37:4

God knows you and your situation perfectly. Remember the principle of grace as you review your week, and don't be hard on yourself.

What mini-goals did I accomplish this week?

_____
_____
_____
_____

What rewards did I enjoy?

_____
_____
_____
_____

What other things did I accomplish this week?

_____
_____
_____
_____

Are there any mini-goals that need to be modified or carried over to next week?

_____
_____
_____
_____

MY MIRACLES: Obstacles I have overcome this week and other ways I have seen God's hand.

_____
_____
_____
_____
_____

Obstacles I have *"given to God"* for further illumination:

_____
_____
_____
_____

NOTES: _____
_____
_____
_____
_____
_____
_____
_____
_____
_____
_____
_____
_____
_____

END OF MONTH SUMMARY

Cast not away therefore your confidence, ... For ye have need of patience, that, after ye have done the will of God, ye might receive the promise

HEBREWS 10:35-36

Fill in your data from this month's weekly goal sheets here.

What mini-goals did I accomplish this month?

_____
_____
_____
_____
_____
_____
_____
_____
_____
_____

What rewards did I enjoy?

_____
_____
_____
_____

What other things did I accomplish this month?

MY MIRACLES: Obstacles I have overcome this month and other ways I have seen God's hand:

How have I changed?

What mini-goals do I want to work on next month to keep moving forward?

Will you please email me at **tamarakandersonauthor@gmail.com** to tell me about your accomplishments this month? I'd love to rejoice with you in your success!

NOTES:

GOALS: WEEK __

*I will instruct thee and teach thee in the way which thou shalt go:
I will guide thee with mine eye.*

PSALM 32:8

My Inspired Resolution: DATE: _____

_____

MINI-GOALS – What I will accomplish this week + reward for each goal:

_____

_____

_____

Now, **talk to God about it**. Tell Him about your weekly goals and ask for courage, faith, and patience to accomplish them.

Begin each morning with prayer. Tell God about your mini-goals and ask for the wisdom and determination to accomplish them. Schedule how you will work on one of your mini-goals that day and do it! Meditate and envision yourself accomplishing each goal and enjoying your reward.

Don't be discouraged if life throws curve balls at you during the day. Life happens. Give yourself grace and keep going. Learn more about how to overcome obstacles on the next page.

End every day with a prayer of thanks and a report of how you have done with your goals that day.

List any additional ideas or thoughts after your prayers below.

_____

_____

_____

Be flexible enough to incorporate additional ideas into your weekly goals. This is how you learn to trust God and be spontaneous enough to walk through doors that come up mid-week.

OBSTACLES: WEEK __

Fight the good fight of faith.
1 TIMOTHY 6:12

During the week, take a few moments to evaluate this question:

What obstacles am I facing? _____

_____
_____
_____
_____

Talk to God at night about these obstacles and ask for His help. Turning it over to God doesn't mean you do nothing, but that you don't need to stress or worry. With God as your partner, you know you just need to do what you are able to do and leave the rest in His hands.

I have had some amazing experiences going to sleep with an obstacle or question and then waking at 4:30am with the answer. I know that between God and our subconscious working on the problem, ideas will come.

When you awake the next morning, before you look at any device, spend time thinking about your obstacle. Keep a prayer in your heart throughout the day and ask God to help you see or hear the solution. Write down any additional ideas or impressions below that may come to you. Then tweak it or find someone who can help you.

_____
_____
_____
_____
_____

Keep working and moving forward. If you find a closed door, trust that God has a better door for you to walk toward and keep your momentum going. You can also shift your focus to another mini goal until you the way opens. Pray and God will guide you.

END OF WEEK SUMMARY: WEEK __

But Jesus beheld them, and said unto them,
With men this is impossible; but with God all things are possible.

MATTHEW 19:26

God knows you and your situation perfectly. Remember the principle of grace as you review your week, and don't be hard on yourself.

What mini-goals did I accomplish this week?

_____
_____
_____
_____

What rewards did I enjoy?

_____
_____
_____
_____

What other things did I accomplish this week?

_____
_____
_____
_____

Are there any mini-goals that need to be modified or carried over to next week?

_____
_____
_____

MY MIRACLES: Obstacles I have overcome this week and other ways I have seen God's hand.

_____
_____
_____
_____
_____

Obstacles I have *"given to God"* for further illumination:

_____
_____
_____
_____

NOTES: _____
_____
_____
_____
_____
_____
_____
_____
_____
_____
_____
_____
_____
_____

GOALS: WEEK ___

And we know that all things work together for good to them that love God, to them who are the called according to his purpose.

ROMANS 8:28

My Inspired Resolution: DATE: _____

MINI-GOALS – What I will accomplish this week + reward for each goal:

Now, **talk to God about it**. Tell Him about your weekly goals and ask for courage, faith, and patience to accomplish them.

Begin each morning with prayer. Tell God about your mini-goals and ask for the wisdom and determination to accomplish them. Schedule how you will work on one of your mini-goals that day and do it! Meditate and envision yourself accomplishing each goal and enjoying your reward.

Don't be discouraged if life throws curve balls at you during the day. Life happens. Give yourself grace and keep going. Learn more about how to overcome obstacles on the next page.

End every day with a prayer of thanks and a report of how you have done with your goals that day.

List any additional ideas or thoughts after your prayers below.

Be flexible enough to incorporate additional ideas into your weekly goals. This is how you learn to trust God and be spontaneous enough to walk through doors that come up mid-week.

OBSTACLES: WEEK __

Ye are of God, little children, and have overcome them:
because greater is he that is in you, than he that is in the world.

1 JOHN 4:4

During the week, take a few moments to evaluate this question:

What obstacles am I facing? _____

_____

_____

_____

_____

Talk to God at night about these obstacles and ask for His help. Turning it over to God doesn't mean you do nothing, but that you don't need to stress or worry. With God as your partner, you know you just need to do what you are able to do and leave the rest in His hands.

I have had some amazing experiences going to sleep with an obstacle or question and then waking at 4:30am with the answer. I know that between God and our subconscious working on the problem, ideas will come.

When you awake the next morning, before you look at any device, spend time thinking about your obstacle. Keep a prayer in your heart throughout the day and ask God to help you see or hear the solution. Write down any additional ideas or impressions below that may come to you. Then tweak it or find someone who can help you.

_____

_____

_____

_____

_____

Keep working and moving forward. If you find a closed door, trust that God has a better door for you to walk toward and keep your momentum going. You can also shift your focus to another mini goal until you the way opens. Pray and God will guide you.

END OF WEEK SUMMARY: WEEK __

Be ye transformed by the renewing of your mind, that ye may prove what is that good, and acceptable, and perfect, will of God.

ROMANS 12:2

God knows you and your situation perfectly. Remember the principle of grace as you review your week, and don't be hard on yourself.

What mini-goals did I accomplish this week?

_____
_____
_____
_____

What rewards did I enjoy?

_____
_____
_____
_____

What other things did I accomplish this week?

_____
_____
_____

Are there any mini-goals that need to be modified or carried over to next week?

_____
_____
_____

MY MIRACLES: Obstacles I have overcome this week and other ways I have seen God's hand.

_____
_____
_____
_____
_____

Obstacles I have *"given to God"* for further illumination:

_____
_____
_____
_____

NOTES: _____

_____
_____
_____
_____
_____
_____
_____
_____
_____
_____
_____
_____
_____

GOALS: WEEK __

But they that wait upon the Lord shall renew their strength; they shall mount up with wings as eagles; they shall run, and not be weary; and they shall walk, and not faint.

ISAIAH 40:31

My Inspired Resolution: DATE: _____

MINI-GOALS – What I will accomplish this week + reward for each goal:

_____

_____

_____

Now, **talk to God about it**. Tell Him about your weekly goals and ask for courage, faith, and patience to accomplish them.

Begin each morning with prayer. Tell God about your mini-goals and ask for the wisdom and determination to accomplish them. Schedule how you will work on one of your mini-goals that day and do it! Meditate and envision yourself accomplishing each goal and enjoying your reward.

Don't be discouraged if life throws curve balls at you during the day. Life happens. Give yourself grace and keep going. Learn more about how to overcome obstacles on the next page.

End every day with a prayer of thanks and a report of how you have done with your goals that day.

List any additional ideas or thoughts after your prayers below.

_____

_____

_____

Be flexible enough to incorporate additional ideas into your weekly goals. This is how you learn to trust God and be spontaneous enough to walk through doors that come up mid-week.

OBSTACLES: WEEK __

O Lord, I beseech thee, send now prosperity.

PSALM 118:25

During the week, take a few moments to evaluate this question:

What obstacles am I facing? _____

_____

_____

_____

_____

Talk to God at night about these obstacles and ask for His help. Turning it over to God doesn't mean you do nothing, but that you don't need to stress or worry. With God as your partner, you know you just need to do what you are able to do and leave the rest in His hands.

I have had some amazing experiences going to sleep with an obstacle or question and then waking at 4:30am with the answer. I know that between God and our subconscious working on the problem, ideas will come.

When you awake the next morning, before you look at any device, spend time thinking about your obstacle. Keep a prayer in your heart throughout the day and ask God to help you see or hear the solution. Write down any additional ideas or impressions below that may come to you. Then tweak it or find someone who can help you.

_____

_____

_____

_____

_____

Keep working and moving forward. If you find a closed door, trust that God has a better door for you to walk toward and keep your momentum going. You can also shift your focus to another mini goal until you the way opens. Pray and God will guide you.

END OF WEEK SUMMARY: WEEK __

Whatsoever things are true, ... honest, ... just, ... pure, ... lovely, ... good report; if there be any virtue, and if there be any praise, think on these things.

PHILIPPIANS 4:8

God knows you and your situation perfectly. Remember the principle of grace as you review your week, and don't be hard on yourself.

What mini-goals did I accomplish this week?

___

What rewards did I enjoy?

___

What other things did I accomplish this week?

___

Are there any mini-goals that need to be modified or carried over to next week?

___

MY MIRACLES: Obstacles I have overcome this week and other ways I have seen God's hand.

_____
_____
_____
_____
_____
_____

Obstacles I have *"given to God"* for further illumination:

_____
_____
_____
_____
_____

NOTES: _____
_____
_____
_____
_____
_____
_____
_____
_____
_____
_____
_____
_____
_____

GOALS: WEEK ___

Great is thy faithfulness. The Lord is my portion, saith my soul; therefore I will hope in him.
LAMENTATIONS 3:23-24

My Inspired Resolution: DATE: _____

MINI-GOALS – What I will accomplish this week + reward for each goal:

Now, **talk to God about it**. Tell Him about your weekly goals and ask for courage, faith, and patience to accomplish them.

Begin each morning with prayer. Tell God about your mini-goals and ask for the wisdom and determination to accomplish them. Schedule how you will work on one of your mini-goals that day and do it! Meditate and envision yourself accomplishing each goal and enjoying your reward.

Don't be discouraged if life throws curve balls at you during the day. Life happens. Give yourself grace and keep going. Learn more about how to overcome obstacles on the next page.

End every day with a prayer of thanks and a report of how you have done with your goals that day.

List any additional ideas or thoughts after your prayers below.

Be flexible enough to incorporate additional ideas into your weekly goals. This is how you learn to trust God and be spontaneous enough to walk through doors that come up mid-week.

OBSTACLES: WEEK __

Thou shalt preserve me from trouble; thou shalt compass me about with songs of deliverance.

PSALM 32:7

During the week, take a few moments to evaluate this question:

What obstacles am I facing? _____

_____

_____

_____

_____

Talk to God at night about these obstacles and ask for His help. Turning it over to God doesn't mean you do nothing, but that you don't need to stress or worry. With God as your partner, you know you just need to do what you are able to do and leave the rest in His hands.

I have had some amazing experiences going to sleep with an obstacle or question and then waking at 4:30am with the answer. I know that between God and our subconscious working on the problem, ideas will come.

When you awake the next morning, before you look at any device, spend time thinking about your obstacle. Keep a prayer in your heart throughout the day and ask God to help you see or hear the solution. Write down any additional ideas or impressions below that may come to you. Then tweak it or find someone who can help you.

_____

_____

_____

_____

_____

Keep working and moving forward. If you find a closed door, trust that God has a better door for you to walk toward and keep your momentum going. You can also shift your focus to another mini goal until you the way opens. Pray and God will guide you.

END OF WEEK SUMMARY: WEEK ___

Jesus saith unto them, My meat is to do the will of him that sent me, and to finish his work.

JOHN 4:34

God knows you and your situation perfectly. Remember the principle of grace as you review your week, and don't be hard on yourself.

What mini-goals did I accomplish this week?

___
___
___
___

What rewards did I enjoy?

___
___
___
___

What other things did I accomplish this week?

___
___
___
___

Are there any mini-goals that need to be modified or carried over to next week?

___
___
___
___

MY MIRACLES: Obstacles I have overcome this week and other ways I have seen God's hand.

Obstacles I have *"given to God"* for further illumination:

NOTES:

GOALS: WEEK __

It is good that a man should both hope and quietly wait for the salvation of the Lord.

LAMENTATIONS 3:26

My Inspired Resolution: DATE: _____

_____

MINI-GOALS – What I will accomplish this week + reward for each goal:

_____

_____

_____

_____

Now, **talk to God about it**. Tell Him about your weekly goals and ask for courage, faith, and patience to accomplish them.

Begin each morning with prayer. Tell God about your mini-goals and ask for the wisdom and determination to accomplish them. Schedule how you will work on one of your mini-goals that day and do it! Meditate and envision yourself accomplishing each goal and enjoying your reward.

Don't be discouraged if life throws curve balls at you during the day. Life happens. Give yourself grace and keep going. Learn more about how to overcome obstacles on the next page.

End every day with a prayer of thanks and a report of how you have done with your goals that day.

List any additional ideas or thoughts after your prayers below.

_____

_____

_____

_____

Be flexible enough to incorporate additional ideas into your weekly goals. This is how you learn to trust God and be spontaneous enough to walk through doors that come up mid-week.

OBSTACLES: WEEK __

And ye shall seek me, and find me, when ye shall search for me with all your heart.

JEREMIAH 29:13

During the week, take a few moments to evaluate this question:

What obstacles am I facing? _____

_____

_____

_____

_____

Talk to God at night about these obstacles and ask for His help. Turning it over to God doesn't mean you do nothing, but that you don't need to stress or worry. With God as your partner, you know you just need to do what you are able to do and leave the rest in His hands.

I have had some amazing experiences going to sleep with an obstacle or question and then waking at 4:30am with the answer. I know that between God and our subconscious working on the problem, ideas will come.

When you awake the next morning, before you look at any device, spend time thinking about your obstacle. Keep a prayer in your heart throughout the day and ask God to help you see or hear the solution. Write down any additional ideas or impressions below that may come to you. Then tweak it or find someone who can help you.

_____

_____

_____

_____

_____

Keep working and moving forward. If you find a closed door, trust that God has a better door for you to walk toward and keep your momentum going. You can also shift your focus to another mini goal until you the way opens. Pray and God will guide you.

END OF WEEK SUMMARY: WEEK __

And all things, whatsoever ye shall ask in prayer, believing, ye shall receive.

MATTHEW 21:22

God knows you and your situation perfectly. Remember the principle of grace as you review your week, and don't be hard on yourself.

What mini-goals did I accomplish this week?

_____
_____
_____
_____

What rewards did I enjoy?

_____
_____
_____
_____

What other things did I accomplish this week?

_____
_____
_____
_____

Are there any mini-goals that need to be modified or carried over to next week?

_____
_____
_____
_____

MY MIRACLES: Obstacles I have overcome this week and other ways I have seen God's hand.

Obstacles I have *"given to God"* for further illumination:

NOTES:

END OF MONTH SUMMARY

The desire accomplished is sweet to the soul.

PROVERBS 13:19

Fill in your data from this month's weekly goal sheets here.

What mini-goals did I accomplish this month?

_____
_____
_____
_____
_____
_____
_____
_____
_____
_____
_____
_____

What rewards did I enjoy?

_____
_____
_____
_____

What other things did I accomplish this month?

MY MIRACLES: Obstacles I have overcome this month and other ways I have seen God's hand:

How have I changed?

What mini-goals do I want to work on next month to keep moving forward?

Will you please email me at **tamarakandersonauthor@gmail.com** to tell me about your accomplishments this month? I'd love to rejoice with you in your success!

NOTES:

END OF FOURTH QUARTER SUMMARY

For I know the thoughts that I think toward you, saith the LORD, thoughts of peace, and not of evil, to give you an expected end.

JEREMIAH 29:11

Fill in your data from this quarter's monthly goal sheets here.　　DATE: _____

What mini-goals did I accomplish this during the last three months?

What rewards did I enjoy?

What other things did I accomoplish?

MY MIRACLES: Obstacles I have overcome during the past 3 months and other ways I have seen God's hand:

How have I changed?

What mini-goals do I want to work on during the next quarter to keep moving forward?

END OF YEAR SUMMARY

*And Stephen, full of faith and power,
did great wonders and miracles among the people.*

ACTS 6:8

Fill in your data from each quarter's monthly goal sheets here.

DATE:

What mini-goals did I accomplish during the last year?

Mini-goals I accomplished during the last year — *continued:*

What rewards did I enjoy?

What other things did I accomoplish this year?

Other things I accomoplished this year — *continued*:

MY MIRACLES: Obstacles I overcame during this year and other ways I have seen God's hand:

MY MIRACLES: Obstacles I overcame during this year and other ways I have seen God's hand – *continued:*

How have I changed?

How have I changed? – *continued*

What mini-goals am I considering as I look at this new year?

Mini-goals am I considering as I look at this new year – *continued*:

MEET THE AUTHOR

Tamara K. Anderson is a speaker, author, podcaster, and musician, whose main focus is to inspire hope and healing through Jesus Christ. Tamara and her husband Justin have four children who are blessed and challenged by autism, ADHD, and mental health issues. Her family is her greatest joy.

Tamara's passion for teaching from the scriptures began when she started college—especially from the life of Jesus Christ. She has used these skills for decades as a Sunday School teacher, and as a missionary.

She received her Bachelor of Science degree and then went on to get advanced degrees from the School of Hard Knocks; the latter proved to be the most challenging, and the most rewarding.

Tamara likes kitchen gadgets, power tools, puttering in her garden, zip-lining, and hiking. She is a sucker for good books and at times can be found awake at 2:00 am to finish a book she just can't put down.

She is the author of *Normal for Me*, her award-winning booklets, *The Mother's Mite*, and *A Broken Down Holiday*. Tamara hosted the podcast, *Stories of Hope in Hard Times*, for four years, and landed in the top 5% of podcasts worldwide. She is the co-host of the *American Mother's Mom-to-Mom Podcast*.

Tamara has moved fourteen times including six states and two countries; she and her family currently live in Utah.

www.ingramcontent.com/pod-product-compliance
Lightning Source LLC
Chambersburg PA
CBHW080321080526
44585CB00021B/2430